Our "Compacted" Compact Clinicals Team

Dear Valued Customer,

Welcome to Compact Clinicals. We are committed to bringing mental health professionals up-to-date diagnostic and treatment information in a compact, timesaving, easy-to-read format. Our **new** line of books provides the most current, thorough reviews of assessment and treatment strategies for mental disorders. These books and tapes will help each practitioner more effectively plan treatment interventions.

We've "compacted" complete information for diagnosing each disorder and comparing how different theoretical orientations approach treatment. Our books use nonacademic language, real-world examples, and well-defined terminology.

Enjoy this and other timesaving books from Compact Clinicals.

Sincerely,

Melanie Dean

Melanie Dean, Ph.D.
President

Compact Clinicals New Line of Books

Compact Clinicals currently offers these condensed reviews for professionals:

- **A Condensed Review of the Changes from DSM-III-R to DSM-IV**

- **Attention Deficit Hyperactivity Disorder (in Adults and Children):** The Latest Assessment and Treatment Strategies (available in book format and audio tape)

- **Borderline Personality Disorder:** The Latest Assessment and Treatment Strategies (available in book format and audio tape)

- **Major Depressive Disorder:** The Latest Assessment and Treatment Strategies (available in book format and audio tape)

- **Conduct Disorders:** The Latest Assessment and Treatment Strategies (available in book format and audio tape)

Call for Writers

Compact Clinicals is always interested in publishing new titles in order to keep our selection of books current and comprehensive. If you have a book proposal or an idea you would like to discuss, please call or write to:

Melanie Dean, Ph.D., President
Compact Clinicals
7205 NW Waukomis Suite A
Kansas City, MO 64151
(816) 587-0044

Attention Deficit Hyperactivity Disorder
(in Adults and Children)

The Latest Assessment and Treatment Strategies

by
Juliet L. Jett, Ph.D.

 Compact Clinicals...*condensed reviews for professionals*

Attention Deficit Hyperactivity Disorder (in Adults and Children) The Latest Assessment and Treatment Strategies

by
Juliet L. Jett, Ph.D.

Published by: Compact Clinicals
7205 NW Waukomis Dr., Suite A
Kansas City, MO. 64151
816-587-0044

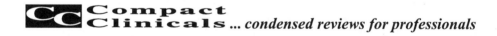

Compact Clinicals ... *condensed reviews for professionals*

Copy Editing and Desktop Publishing by:
      In Plain English
      P.O. Box 1309
      Salt Lake City, UT. 84091
Cover Design by:
      Patrick G. Handley

Library of Congress Catalogue Card Number: 96-83589
ISBN 1-887537-07-4

Read Me First

As a mental health professional, often the information you need can only be obtained after countless hours of reading or library research. If your schedule precludes this time commitment, Compact Clinicals is the answer.

Our books and tapes are practitioner oriented with easy-to-read treatment descriptions and examples. Compact Clinicals books are written in a nonacademic style. Our books are formatted to make the first reading as well as ongoing reference quick and easy. You will find:

- *Anecdotes*—Each chapter begins and ends with a fictionalized account that personalizes the disorder. These accounts include a **"Dear Diary"** entry at the beginning of each chapter that illustrates a typical client's viewpoint about their disorder. Each chapter ends with **"File Notes"** of a fictional therapist, Pat Owen. These **"File Notes"** address assessment, diagnosis, and treatment considerations for the "client writing" the **"Dear Diary"** entries.

- *Sidebars*—Narrow columns on the outside of each page highlight important information, preview upcoming sections or concepts, and define terms used in the text.

- *Definitions*—Terms are defined in the sidebars where they originally appear in the text and in an alphabetical glossary on pages 83 through 86.

- *References*—Numbered references appear in the text following information from that source. Full references appear in a bibliography on pages 87 through 92.

- *Case Examples*—Our examples illustrate typical client comments or conversational exchanges that help clarify different treatment approaches. Identifying information in the examples (e.g., the individual's real name, profession, age, and/or location) has been changed to protect the confidentiality of those clients discussed in case examples.

Contents

Diary of Todd J.

January 26

Mom is taking me to see some doctor today. I guess I'm getting on her nerves lately. It doesn't help that I broke that lamp yesterday. It sure bugs her when I don't listen and don't finish anything. Seems like those other kids can pay attention a whole lot better than me. Sometimes I just don't get what the teacher is talking about cause I can't stand having to sit still and do nothing. Maybe this doctor can help me do better at school.

You will be following a typical client's thoughts about their disorder through the "Dear Diary" notes at the beginning of each chapter. At the end of each chapter, a fictional therapist's "File Notes" will reflect the assessment and treatment of the client writing the "Dear Diary" notes.

Chapter 1: Overview of the Disorder

What is Attention Deficit Hyperactivity Disorder (ADHD)?

ADHD is one of the most commonly diagnosed mental disorders of children, accounting for 30-40 percent of all referrals made to child guidance clinics.[1,2,3] In addition, this same disorder accounts for a significant percentage of recent referrals in adult treatment settings.

Those who suffer from ADHD typically present symptoms grouped as either those related to inattentiveness, those related to hyperactivity, or a combination or both.

- *Inattentive symptoms* seen in children with ADHD include making careless mistakes and moving rapidly from activity to activity. They have difficulty listening to others, following instructions, or completing tasks. These children often avoid tasks that require prolonged attention, are forgetful, and can easily be distracted during activities.

- *Hyperactive characteristics* include high levels of activity and impulsive symptoms. Children with these ADHD symptoms tend to be very restless. They speak out of turn by butting into conversations or blurting out comments inappropriately. In addition, they have difficulty waiting turns, being patient, and/or playing quietly. The Diagnostic and Statistical Manual of Mental Disorders (DSM) has historically considered this hyperactivity (or impulsivity) sufficient for an ADHD diagnosis. The latest edition, DSM-IV, now lists prominent hyperactive symptoms as a subgroup of the disorder.[1]

Frequently those with ADHD present a combination of the two sets of symptoms.

This chapter answers the following:

- **What is Attention Deficit Hyperactivity Disorder (ADHD)?—** *This section presents two very distinct sets of symptoms. Each of these or the combination of the symptoms can represent ADHD. This section also discusses core symptoms about which researchers seem to agree.*

- **What are the "Knowns" and "Unknowns" About ADHD?—** *This section reviews those areas that reflect consensus as well as those that reflect conflict in our current state of knowledge about the disorder.*

- **How Common is ADHD?—** *This section presents prevalence rates among children and adults.*

- **Will Children with ADHD "Grow Out of It?"—** *This section highlights research on whether or not those with ADHD will continue experiencing symptoms through adolescence and into adulthood.*

According to most clinicians and researchers, ADHD core symptoms include:[3,4,5]

1. ***Short Attention Span***—This brief attentional focus is often frustrating to others, such as when a child is up, down, and all over a chair while watching television; or when a teacher has to repeat instructions over and over. A "normal" child might play a single game while the child with ADHD might play with five or six different games or toys within the same time period. An adult may act disinterested in or avoid activities requiring concentration, such as movies, books, painting, or sewing.

2. ***Distractibility***—This occurs when stimuli in the environment attract attention away from the task at hand. For example, a child who attempts to take out the trash may be distracted along the way by the dog, a younger brother, a toy, or something interesting in the trash. As a result, the trash never makes it to the garbage can. An adult may demonstrate distractibility by never finishing tasks when interrupted by phone calls or comments by coworkers.

3. ***Impulsivity***—Impulsivity involves acting without thinking and at times can be dangerous. Examples include interrupting somebody while they're talking, running into the street without looking, jumping off a roof because it "looked fun," or jumping ahead of others' turn during a game. An adult may impulse buy, or make decisions on the spot, without thinking through consequences.

4. ***Inability to Fit in With Peers***—This core symptom stems from poorly developed social skills due to poor judgment that results from inattention and impulsivity. Not waiting for a turn and difficulty remembering and obeying rules are problems that typically occur among children. Adults may have trouble with coworkers or may change jobs frequently due to disagreements with employers.

What Are the "Knowns" and "Unknowns" About ADHD?

Although ADHD is a common mental disorder, researchers and clinicians find it to be one of the greatest unsolved mysteries of modern mental health.

ADHD's different presentations make it difficult for experts to define the disorder. In fact, continuing controversy exists as to whether ADHD is one disorder or a spectrum of different disorders. Our understanding of the syndrome has changed radically over time.[6] The definition of the disorder has shifted back and forth from a disorder with a neurological basis to one that is characterized only by behavioral differences.

The first description of hyperactive symptoms was a description of "Fidgety Phil's" behaviors in 1854.

Clinicians have characterized the disorder as "organic drivenness," "minimal brain dysfunction," "hyperkinetic syndrome," "attention deficit disorder," and (most recently) "attention deficit hyperactivity disorder."[6]

In addition, there is conflicting evidence regarding the origin of the disorder. For example, although neurological difficulties account for many of those diagnosed with ADHD, the role of family dysfunction, brain differences, and environmental factors varies from one individual to another. (See chapter three for a related discussion.)

Due to the change in criteria for ADHD during the history of the disorder, many people diagnosed with ADHD may not meet current criteria. In addition, many who have not been previously diagnosed may now qualify for the label of ADHD.[2]

Few studies have assessed the effects of ADHD over the long term or in natural settings. In addition, the variability in definition, criterion, and etiology used in past research has resulted in some contradictory and confusing results regarding the origin and treatment of ADHD.[7]

Our current state of knowledge about the disorder involves almost universal consensus on:

- The core symptoms of the disorder

- How common ADHD is among children and the increase in adult diagnosis

Throughout the diagnostic and treatment sections of this book (chapters 2 and 3), you will find detailed information on research conducted to better define ADHD etiology and develop effective treatment methodologies.

Thousands of research articles have been written about ADHD during the past 20 years.

The problem for researchers and clinicians involves these perplexing "unknowns" about ADHD:

- Whether ADHD is one disorder or represents a spectrum of disorders.

- Conflicting evidence exists as to the disorder's origin.

- Researchers have a great deal of difficulty defining the role of ADHD in adulthood.

Because of these "unknowns," ADHD continues to be one of the most popular subject areas for research, due in part to the:

- Severity and chronic nature of the condition

- Popularity of stimulant drugs as an easily researched intervention

- Multi-disciplinary interest generated by psychiatrists, neurologists, psychologists, educators, pediatricians, and biochemists

How Common Is ADHD?

ADHD is one of the most commonly diagnosed mental disorders of children and has become more prevalent in adults as researchers continually clarify diagnostic methods and definitions. Several studies found that two to five percent of school-aged children presented well-defined and pervasive symptoms of ADHD. This means that between one and three million children suffer from the disorder at any one point in time.

The consistency of defined ADHD prevalence rates relies on consistent definitions used for diagnosis. For example, those studies that found ADHD prevalence rates ranging from two to five percent in school-aged children were based on:[8,9,7]

- Diagnostic techniques that used multiple reports from parents, teachers, physicians, and others to determine the pervasiveness of ADHD-related behavior

- Studies of clients who presented well-defined symptoms

Prevalence also seems to relate to gender differences. Researchers estimate that boys are 3-10 times more affected with the disorder than girls.[8,9] However, some studies such as one that targeted self-referred adult populations found that those studied represented more even distributions between men and women than research on children. Since ADHD is diagnosed only if symptoms were reported in childhood, the higher percentage of females diagnosed as adults than as children may indicate that referral sources notice more overt behavioral disturbances (i.e., Conduct Disorder, Oppositional Defiant Disorder) in boys than in girls.[10]

Speculation exists that gender differences in prevalence research may partially reflect differences in the level of disruption to others rather than actual gender differences in ADHD prevalence.

Another study that supports this theory found that girls with ADHD showed greater impairment in cognitive functioning, school achievement, and peer interactions than "normal" peers (those with less noticeable problems). Girls also tended to be older when referred.[11]

Will Children with ADHD "Grow Out of It?"

The role of ADHD in adulthood is even less understood than the disorder's origin. Good evidence exists that many people continue to have problems through adolescence and even as adults.

Research suggests that about 70 percent of children diagnosed with ADHD show signs of the disorder into adolescence.[3,12] One study in particular found that those adolescents without continuing signs of the disorder functioned the same as their "normal" peers.[14] However, those who continue to show symptoms appear to have a 50 percent chance of having a coexisting conduct disorder. Two-thirds of these adolescents are likely to have a substance abuse disorder sometime in their lives.

Disorders coexisting with ADHD, especially those associated with conduct and antisocial problems, are predictors of greater disturbance in adulthood.[13]

According to some studies, about 25 percent of youths with ADHD drop out of high school.[14,7] Continuing school problems could be partially explained by the nature of such a structured setting. For instance, teachers of the last grade completed by those with ADHD consistently rated those students as inferior to others in areas such as task completion, working independently, getting along with others, and punctuality.[7] These results may be due to the specific skills

It is possible that a student's difficulty with these tasks may contribute to early school withdrawal common for this group.

necessary for performance in a school situation. Schools typically require extended listening, organization, and rote memorization.

Adults with ADHD present the same basic sets of symptoms as children but may behave differently. For example, adults with ADHD may:

- Change jobs frequently

Job changes and extra work (such as second jobs or hobbies) are options for coping with the feelings, perceptions, and needs experienced by those with ADHD.

- Have difficulty sustaining attention on tedious or boring tasks

- Be easily distracted away from important tasks by just the slightest interruption or new stimuli

- Make impulsive decisions related to spending money, travel, jobs, or social plans

These adults tend to talk rapidly, change the subject during conversation and then change it back again, and they may interrupt others impulsively. They prefer jobs and tasks that are varied and active rather than steady and sedate. They are also more likely to have dropped out of school early and to remember school very negatively.

There appears to be little difference in outcome (prognosis) between males and females with ADHD. However, males are at greater risk for Conduct Disorder, and prognosis is poor for those with both ADHD and Conduct Disorder.[13]

Researchers estimate that 30-50 percent of adults diagnosed with ADHD during childhood will continue to have problems.[3,15,7] About one-third to one-half of adults diagnosed with ADHD report symptoms acute enough to cause impairment in daily functioning.[8,13,7] Often, those who have symptomatic problems make frequent job changes and demonstrate poor work performance. They tend to suffer from:

- Feelings of impatience

- Perceptions of tasks as repetitive and uninteresting over time

- The need to fill inactive time to avoid restlessness or boredom

In general, adults with a childhood diagnosis of ADHD are different than "normal" peers in several ways.[14,16,7] According to recent long-term studies, these adults typically do not complete formal schooling: only about 75 percent graduate from high school, and very few complete college. Although they are as likely to be employed as those without ADHD, their work status tends to be lower, associated to some extent with their level of education.

Some mental disorders are more prevalent among adults with ADHD, especially Antisocial Personality Disorder and Substance Abuse Disorders. These disorders occur much more frequently in those who continue to experience disturbance in the areas of attention, impulsivity, and hyperactivity.

Although questions have been raised in the past regarding an association between anxiety and ADHD, there was no difference in the incidence of anxiety disorders between adults with a history of ADHD and their peers.

Those who do not show impairment and function well in their daily environment may do so for a number of reasons. Symptoms may remit over time, ending the disruptive influence and impairment. Environmental changes that occur when someone transitions from student to working adult may also play a part, since home and work environments can be more varied for adults than children. An adult's choices can be timed to their individual needs, rather than to a parent's or teacher's set schedule. One study found a much higher percentage of those with childhood ADHD managing their own businesses.[14] This could be a result of these people's ability to utilize unique skills and energies, or it could result from their inability to maintain a regular job.

In one study, young adults with ADHD (ages 18-22) experienced no overall differences in employer ratings of work performance or frequency of employment. They did, however, experience more frequent job changes, worked several part-time jobs, and became dissatisfied more easily as time went on.[7] After several years of employment, employers rated work performance as inferior for those with ADHD in areas such as completing tasks and working independently. Employer ratings of punctuality and good working relationships remained similar to non-ADHD workers. The results from this study also indicated no significant difference in average annual income despite changes in work performance over time.

Work settings may allow freedom of movement and self-pacing. In some instances, the variety afforded by the workplace may increase productivity.

*Therapy Notes
from the Desk of
Pat Owen*

Forty-two year old mother (S.J.) brought her 11 year old son (T.J) in for an evaluation. She reports that his grades have been steadily dropping at school, that he doesn't seem to pay attention at home or school, and that he can't seem to be still and concentrate on any-thing except video games. She reports typical behaviors like going from a walk to a run, having never needed a nap as a small child, and that he "doesn't seem to want to do his work." He has been fighting more at school. The mother has been getting more complaints from his teacher that he is disruptive in the classroom by being "wound up," "vocal," "a trouble maker," and "always out of his chair."

Sounds like ADHD, but need to gather more information through a formal assessment and rule out Conduct Disorder and Mood Disorder.

Chapter Two: Diagnosing Attention Deficit Hyperactivity Disorder

---

Diary of Todd J.

March 13

The doctor thinks that I have ADHD. She asked me and my mom a whole lot of questions. She asked all about how much trouble I've been in. My teacher even had to fill out a paper. I was really embarrassed, but Mom says it will help me get better. The doctor wants me to start taking some pills for this; she says it will help my squirminess and make me pay attention better. Maybe I will be able to think better at school.

This chapter will answer the following:

- **What is the Latest DSM-IV Criteria for Diagnosing ADHD?**— This section features a reprint of current DSM-IV criteria for diagnosing ADHD as well as a discussion of changes from DSM-III-R.

- **What are Typical Characteristics of those with ADHD?**— This section discusses ADHD symptoms present at different developmental stages, from infancy to adulthood.

- **What Assessment Techniques can be Used to Diagnose ADHD?**— This section covers interview techniques, observation techniques, and psychometric assessment tools that can distinguish ADHD from other disorders.

- **What Differentiates ADHD from other Disorders?**— This section presents nine disorders or symptom areas that must be differentiated from ADHD for accurate diagnosis.

Diagnosing ADHD requires careful assessment processes to rule out a host of mental, physical, situational, and genetic disorders that could present a similar picture. Clinicians should pay careful attention to:

- Family and medical histories.

- Possible physical and genetic causes for the behavior. (Because several physical disorders have similar symptoms, each child and adult must be evaluated by a physician.)

- Possible existence of other mental disorders through self-report and psychometric assessments.

- Analysis of a child's symptoms presented in settings where the child can be observed with "normal" peers. Although this approach helps to distinguish behaviors that vary significantly from other children, no definitive measures exist to differentiate "normal" from ADHD behavior.

Diagnosing ADHD in an adult is particularly difficult because symptoms must have begun before age seven. This is particularly troublesome to verify as childhood histories may be suspect. Repeated studies have indicated poor recollection of past events, moods, and behaviors, especially when evaluating the degree of intensity. There is even some evidence that parental recall is better than that of the adult client.[17,14] Because contact with an adult's family members is often impossible, asking for and interpreting historical information requires extreme care.

To assist clinicians with the difficult task of diagnosing ADHD, this chapter will cover:

- How DSM-IV organizes the various criteria for diagnosis into two subtypes and carefully defines pervasiveness

- How DSM-IV criteria differs from DSM-III-R criteria

- Typical ADHD characteristics the clinician can watch for in infants, preschoolers, grade-school-aged children, adolescents, and adults

- Varied assessment tools available for testing those who present ADHD symptoms

- Other mental and genetic disorders that can be differentiated from ADHD

What is the Latest DSM-IV Criteria for Diagnosing ADHD?

The <u>Diagnostic and Statistical Manual of Mental Disorders,</u> Fourth Edition (DSM-IV) presents the latest ADHD definition. DSM-IV clarifies symptom definitions and addresses the debate over the role of hyperactivity by including this symptom as a subtype rather than a necessary diagnostic component. DSM-IV organizes ADHD criteria into two subtypes: [1]

- Symptoms of inattention, distractibility, and disorganization

- Behavioral problems with hyperactivity and impulsivity

To control over-diagnosis, new DSM-IV criteria are quite stringent, especially in terms of symptom pervasiveness. These criteria emphasize that to diagnose ADHD, the client must:

- Demonstrate impairment in social, academic, or occupational functioning
- Demonstrate significant *dysfunction* for the person's age and developmental level
- *Manifest symptoms* prior to age seven; many symptoms persist for a period of at least six months
- Present symptoms in two or more situations (e.g., work, school, home, or in the community)

dysfunction— a disruption in normal functioning

manifest symptoms— overtly display symptoms

DSM-IV Criteria

DSM-IV Criteria for Attention Deficit Hyperactivity Disorder[1]

"A. Six (or more) of either 1) Inattention, or 2) Hyperactivity-Impulsivity. Symptoms must have persisted for at least 6 months to a degree that is maladaptive and inconsistent with developmental level:

1) Inattention:

a) often fails to give close attention to details or makes careless mistakes in school-work, work, or other activities

b) often has difficulty sustaining attention in tasks or play activities

c) often does not seem to listen when spoken to directly

d) often does not follow through on instructions and fails to finish schoolwork, chores, or duties in the workplace (not due to oppositional behavior or failure to understand instructions)

e) often has difficulty organizing tasks and activities

f) often avoids, dislikes, or is reluctant to engage in tasks that require sustained mental effort (such as schoolwork or homework)

g) often loses things necessary for tasks or activities (e.g. toys, school assignments, pencils, books, or tools)

(Continued on Page 12)

(DSM-IV Criteria, Continued)

h) is often easily distracted by extraneous stimuli

i) is often forgetful in daily activities

2) Hyperactivity-impulsivity:

Hyperactivity

a) often fidgets with hands or feet or squirms in seat
b) often leaves seat in classroom or in other situations in which remaining seated is expected
c) often runs about or climbs excessively in situations in which it is inappropriate (in adolescents or adults, may be limited to subjective feelings of restlessness)
d) often has difficulty playing or engaging in leisure activities quietly
e) is often "on the go" or often acts as if "driven by a motor"
f) often talks excessively

Impulsivity

g) often blurts out answers before questions have been completed
h) often has difficulty awaiting turn
i) often interrupts or intrudes on others (e.g., butts into conversations or games)

B. Some symptoms causing impairment were present before age 7 years.

C. Some impairment from the symptoms is present in two or more settings (e.g., at school [or work] and at home).

D. There must be clear evidence of clinically significant impairment in social, academic, or occupational functioning.

E. Occurrence is not exclusively during the course of a Pervasive Developmental Disorder, Schizophrenia, or other Psychotic Disorder and are not better accounted for by another mental disorder

Types:

Combined Type:
if both Criteria A1 and A2 are met for the past 6 months

Predominantly Inattentive:
if only Criterion A1 is met (not A2) for the past 6 months

(Continued on Page 13)

(DSM-IV Criteria, Continued)

Predominantly Hyperactive-Impulsive Type:
if only Criterion A2 is met (not A1) for the past 6 months

Not Otherwise Specified:
if there are prominent symptoms of inattention or hyperactivity-impulsivity that do not meet full criteria for ADHD."

(Reprinted with permission by the American Psychiatric Association: <u>Diagnostic and Statistical Manual of Mental Disorders, Fourth Edition.</u> Washington, DC, American Psychiatric Association, 1994)

Differences Between DSM-III-R and DSM-IV Diagnostic Criteria

Changes from DSM-III-R reflect the results of literature reviews, reanalysis of research, and clinical field trials. The DSM-IV integrates ADHD and Undifferentiated ADHD (from the DSM-III-R) into one disorder with different predominating symptom patterns.[18,1] To better define ADHD, DSM-IV increased symptom precision and included hyperactivity as a subtype rather than as necessary criteria for diagnosis.

Other specific changes include:

- Items are no longer listed in descending order of *discriminating power*.

- Criteria have been split into two sections that describe inattention or hyperactivity-impulsivity.

- DSM-IV provides more diagnostic criteria with more detail than DSM-III-R.

- Clinicians are no longer required to code the severity of the disorder (e.g., mild, moderate, or severe).

- Criteria wording has been modified for adults (e.g., the words "work" or "job" have been added to situational descriptions that previously addressed only "play" or "school.")

*discriminating power—
listed in order of ability to differentiate one disorder from another*

- Individuals who currently have symptoms but who no longer meet the full DSM-IV criteria are referred to as being, "In Partial Remission."

- DSM-IV established the category, ADHD Not Otherwise Specified, for atypical cases, such as those who currently fail to meet the full criteria and have not been diagnosed in the past. This category can also be used for those with subthreshold levels of disturbance.

- DSM-IV criteria still include excessive physical activity, but no longer mention an associated "element of danger." The "element of danger" does not adequately discriminate ADHD from other disorders.

What are Typical Characteristics of Those with ADHD?

Those with ADHD present different symptoms depending on whether they are infants, preschoolers, grade-school -aged children, adolescents, or adults.

Although the primary symptoms of ADHD are similar, certain symptoms are more prominent during certain age spans and developmental levels ranging from infancy into adulthood. The following addresses typical symptoms presented by those with ADHD in a clinical setting at various developmental stages.

ADHD Presentation in Infancy

Because ADHD symptoms appear after infancy (generally at three to four years), therapists learn about early symptoms from parents' recollections (accuracy is less certain). One study reported that parents of approximately one-third of the children diagnosed with ADHD remembered difficulties with excessive crying, sleep and feeding problems, and disturbed interactive behaviors. For instance, many parents described their children during infancy as:[7]

- Crying frequently and being difficult to soothe

- Having sleep disturbances such as being excessively drowsy and unresponsive, or sleeping poorly due to over-reactivity and restlessness

- Experiencing feeding difficulties because of irregular appetites, "picky eating," poor sucking or crying to an extent that interfered with nutritional intake

Additional research found delayed development of motor and attentional skills among infants later diagnosed with ADHD.[3]

ADHD Presentation at Preschool Age

Three- and four-year-old children have a pattern of inattention and overactivity that may or may not be related to ADHD. One study indicated that both symptom degree and duration (six to 12 months) are important factors for diagnosis. At this age, therapists may need to evaluate symptoms over a longer period of time than that required by DSM-IV criteria to determine whether or not the behaviors will be outgrown.[3] **Significant diagnostic signs include:**

The disorder may first manifest itself prior to school age; however, it is often first noticed when a child enters a social situation, such as day care or school.

- **Motor restlessness** (the child is always on the go or described as "driven by a motor"; climbs on and gets into things constantly)

- **Insatiable curiosity**

- **Vigorous and sometimes destructive play** (accidental breakage of toys and household objects occurs regularly; accidental injuries are common)

- **Demanding of parental attention**

- **Low-level compliance** (especially with boys)

- **Excessive temper tantrums** (those that far exceed those of "normal" children in frequency, severity, and duration)

- **Difficulty completing developmental tasks** (such as toilet training)

- **Decreased and/or restless sleep**

- **Delays in motor or language development**

- **Family difficulties** (including obtaining and keeping baby sitters, especially with children with severe problems)

Most referrals for ADHD assessment occur during the first, second, and third grades of schooling.

ADHD Presentation During Middle Childhood (ages 6-12)

During these years, children face new demands to fit in and meet school expectations of sitting still, following structure, and sharing one teacher's attention with perhaps 30 other students. Those with ADHD may:

- Be easily distracted
- Engage in off-task activities
- Be unable to sustain attention
- Be impulsive
- Display aggression

reinforcement—any consequence that increases the frequency of the preceding behavior

These behaviors may be exacerbated by the structured, rote nature of many school tasks. For instance, a child may feel that assigned tasks are too difficult, too easy, or too boring which leads to inconsistent *reinforcement* inadequate for learning.

Teachers view children with ADHD as disruptive to classroom flow. The children that escape notice at this stage are usually those whose academic performance is adequate and/or whose symptoms are primarily inattentive rather than disruptive.

Children diagnosed with ADHD during middle childhood often begin to experience a pattern of academic and social failure that leads to poor self-esteem and depression.[3,7] For example, impulsivity can result in poor motivation and underachievement. Children manifest behavioral impulsivity by calling out in class, fidgeting, and repeatedly leaving their seat or getting up "just to check something." They demonstrate cognitive impulsivity by making frequent mistakes, being disorganized, and producing sloppy work.

ADHD symptoms interfere with the child's ability to conform to class rules, participate in cooperative learning, and gain basic reading and writing skills. Delays in motor development and the presence of specific learning disabilities compound children's difficulty in mastering tasks.

Hyperactivity, impulsivity, and inattention interfere with the child's ability to socialize with teachers and peers. Children with ADHD are usually unpopular with peers because they are unable to:

- Wait for their turns
- Remember and follow rules
- Avoid being "poor losers" at games
- Curb their quick tempers

ADHD Presentation in Adolescence

As children reach adolescence, their hyperactivity and impulsivity decrease while attentional skills typically increase.[3,7] Most adolescents with ADHD continue to show impairment in these areas and demonstrate other problem behaviors, such as:

- Discipline problems
- Difficulty with authority
- Significant lags in academic performance
- Poor peer relationships

Adolescents with residual ADHD symptoms typically perform tasks unevenly. For instance, they may burst with creativity for one class project, then forget to do their homework. Adolescents with ADHD are more likely to quit school before graduation.

Diagnosis can be problematic at this phase of a person's development. Clinicians frequently diagnose adolescents with ADHD as having Oppositional Defiant Disorder or Conduct Disorder. The client's attentional disorder may have begun earlier in life and may coexist with the antisocial behaviors. By emphasizing antisocial problems, adolescents whose relationships are already strained with parents, teachers, and peers face being further stigmatized.

Adolescents with ADHD exhibit antisocial behavior and substance abuse more often than "normal" populations, although the degree and severity varies widely.

See the discussion of differential diagnosis on pages 33 through 37 for further clarification.

ADHD Presentation in Adulthood

As children with ADHD reach adulthood, symptoms may decrease. Although the target symptoms of hyperactivity, inattention, and impulsivity are still reported by many clients, only one-third to one-half report levels high enough to cause impairment in daily functioning.[19,8,13,7] At least 50 percent are able to maintain jobs and relationships.

Adults with an extensive history of ADHD who have experienced failure situations at school, home, and in peer relationships find that working and separating from families allows life-style choices that may better suit their needs.[3,8] For instance, individuals labeled as failures because they can't sit still and listen well, may succeed as motivational speakers. Alternatively, another individual may be so mired in their

Major life changes in adulthood make predicting outcome for those with ADHD more difficult.

Adults with ADHD may work well in structured situations, but have difficulty structuring themselves. They may have difficulty with time management and scheduling or may take on more tasks than they can finish. Adults with ADHD also may develop hobbies or pursue work with a high level of stimulation or danger, such as driving race cars, skydiving, or flying.

image of failure that when they tackle jobs requiring skills they don't have, they perpetuate their image of impairment and a continued sense of failure.

Some theorists believe that those with ADHD commit more antisocial acts or have a greater chance of being diagnosed with Antisocial Personality Disorder (APD). Research only supports an association between ADHD and APD in 20 to 30 percent of cases.[14] However, recent research studies using more precise definitions of ADHD and APD found no significant link between the two.[20,21] There is also some indication that alcohol or other substance abuse disorders are more common in adults with ADHD.[14,20]

About half of the adults diagnosed with ADHD in childhood continue to have difficulty as adults. They suffer mild disturbances (e.g., residual ADHD, anxiety symptoms, or sexual problems) more frequently than severe problems (e.g., APD) which occur in only a small percentage of those studied.[20] However, as they mature, those with ADHD generally learn coping or compensation skills. Thus, they may be able to concentrate or curb impulses, but this takes energy away from other areas. In response, they may be rigid or easily frustrated.

What Assessment Techniques Can Be Used to Diagnose ADHD?

Assessing ADHD in children is a multistep process that includes a combination of interview, observation, and the use of psychometric assessment tools.[20,3,22,5] This process is especially important because there is no definitive ADHD diagnosis and no psychological or neurological tests that clearly demarcate "normal" from ADHD behavior. Although ADHD behaviors frequently stand out, clinicians must evaluate the difference between those behaviors and the behavior of same-aged peers to make a distinct diagnosis.

Assessing ADHD in adults is similar to the multistep approach taken for children and adolescents; however, more emphasis is put on self-report techniques and less on observation and standardized measures. Since symptoms are often not as prominent in adulthood, more subtle interview questions may reveal pertinent information. For example, clinicians should ask questions about whether it "feels" hard to sit still, rather than asking about "squirming," or asking if adults seem to have more energy than others they know, rather than asking about excessive energy.

The following pages address the following assessment techniques:

- Interview techniques
- Observation techniques
- Standardized assessment measures

Interview Techniques

Client and parent interviews are the most important methods of assessing ADHD in children. Therapists need to gather a complete social, medical, and developmental history (from conception to present) to differentiate between situational problems, other diagnoses, and ADHD. When compiling this history, ask for specific examples of each characteristic and its impact on daily functioning. These examples help determine whether or not there is a marked difference between the client and normal peers.

In compiling an effective client history, therapists need to thoroughly investigate:

- School or Job Performance
- Family and Individual Psychiatric Histories
- Medical and Developmental History

School or Job Performance

When using interview techniques with a child, gather parent and teacher input about school performance in addition to the child's self-report. Grades and report cards often provide significant ADHD-related indicators of difficulty with skill mastery or problems with organization, impulsivity, or attention. Teacher comments such as, "Joe is always late and loses materials," or "Joe could do better if he listened more and sat still," frequently point out:

- Attention and organizational deficits
- Questionable behaviors related to peer relationships

Thorough interview techniques determine whether the client's behavior differs significantly from "normal" peers. For example, a child who has "difficulty following through on instructions from others" may do so only:

- *In certain situations (school, doing chores)*
- *With certain individuals (parents or employers)*
- *When instructions are complex*

Appendix A features an interview protocol covering these content areas.

Educational and/or psychological testing can clarify how learning disorders impair school performance and differentiate these learning disorders from ADHD.

- Cognitive skill deficits
- The child's inability to coexist and learn with other children

Children with ADHD experience difficulty with peers because they lack social skills and have problems obeying rules (impulsivity) during play activities.

For adults, frequent job changes, missed deadlines, or difficulty completing tasks or ideas may reflect attention deficits. Supervisors and coworkers generally describe problems with adults having interpersonal difficulties and poor social skills. Those with ADHD may also demonstrate extreme creativity or bursts of energy in completing certain tasks.

Family and Individual Psychiatric Histories

Mental disorders with symptoms similar to ADHD include Bipolar Disorder, Conduct Disorder, affective disorders, depressive mood disorder, learning disabilities, anxiety disorders, and Borderline Personality Disorder. See pages 33 through 37 for differential diagnostic information.

Clients may be at risk for ADHD if their relatives have had ADHD or psychiatric, learning, conduct, or developmental disorders. Family history data can also help clarify alternative diagnoses for the ADHD client. For instance, someone whose parents have both been diagnosed with ADHD will more likely be diagnosed with ADHD. A client with one parent diagnosed with Bipolar Disorder may be demonstrating manic symptoms rather than those associated with ADHD.

In children, causal factors may also be related to how well family members currently function. For example, a child's symptoms may relate, in part, to a chaotic home life (due to marital conflict, alcohol abuse, physical or sexual abuse, or psychiatric illness in a family member).

Psychiatric histories should include an assessment of:

- Depression
- Mania
- Anxiety
- Thought or perceptual disturbances

This assessment will help determine what diagnoses may be differential versus coexisting (i.e., are you seeing symptoms of a single disorder or does the client have multiple disorders at the same time.)

Medical and Developmental History

Clinicians should gather a thorough medical and developmental history to point out causal factors that may stem from certain medical conditions, as well as to establish any pattern of ADHD *maladaptive behavior.*[4,5] From a medical standpoint, there are several risk factors associated with ADHD which should be noted by the clinician, including prenatal and postnatal difficulties, maternal substance abuse, and poor maternal health. Even though research on a direct connection between these predisposing factors and ADHD is inconclusive, the therapist should look for these factors when completing the assessment process. The presence of these predisposing factors may help confirm a diagnosis; however, these alone are not enough evidence to make an ADHD diagnosis.

maladaptive behavior–behavior that leads to excessive distress, typically requiring therapy.

Children with certain medical conditions, such as hyperthyroidism, seizures, or allergies (e.g., those allergic to corn, peanuts, or milk), or various genetic disorders, can have symptoms that mimic ADHD symptoms; these conditions could also cause the ADHD symptoms. These problems may already have been treated by a physician or may need investigation. Although by no means definitive signs, several physical factors are associated with ADHD. These factors include:

Certain physical disorders can have symptoms similar to ADHD. These include Fetal Alcohol Syndrome, Pervasive Developmental Disorder, and Neurofibromatosis. Children with various genetic disorders, such as Turner Syndrome and Fragile X syndrome, can also present ADHD type symptoms. For more information, see page 37.

- Left-handedness
- Multiple ear infections
- Headaches
- Frequent illnesses
- Poor hand-eye coordination
- Bed-wetting
- Being accident prone

From a developmental standpoint, parents often report signs of hyperactivity before birth as excessive fetal activity (especially in the third trimester) and early labor. As babies, these children attain developmental milestones erratically in language, motor, or social skills (e.g., walking, talking, or interactive play). Some skills may be acquired early; others are delayed. For example, parents may report that their child "went from a crawl to a run" when starting to walk, but did not speak in full sentences until much later than siblings. ADHD children may sleep less and quit taking naps early. Parents find them difficult to manage as they constantly move from one activity to the next, and their toys never last because of vigorous play and accidents.[8,23]

Utilizing a Specific Interview Format

The most widely used interview format for children was developed by Barkley.[3] The questionnaire includes over 88 questions grouped according to the following:

- Developmental Factors
- Medical History
- Treatment History
- Social History
- Current Behavioral Concerns
- Diagnostic Criteria for ADHD and other disorders
- Other Concerns (related to differential diagnosis)
- Family History

This interview assigns values to most of the responses. Although no specific scoring system exists, higher numbers on certain sections generally reflect the presence of greater risk factors and may highlight areas for further investigation.

An updated version of Barkley's interview has been included as appendix A. Updates to this questionnaire involve revisions to the diagnostic criteria section to reflect DSM-IV. This section lists DSM-IV criteria for ADHD and a variety of psychiatric diagnoses to aid in differential diagnosis. The number of criteria needed to meet a diagnosis follows each section; however, diagnostic decisions cannot be made based solely on meeting the number given on the list. These lists do not cover all requirements for a given diagnosis, but they can be used to pinpoint areas where further exploration will help solidify the diagnosis. The answers given to questions on school history and other concerns may also require further investigation.

Questions for the Adult Interview

Since overt symptoms of inattention, impulsivity, and hyperactivity generally abate by adulthood, the clinician should focus more on behaviors, thoughts, and feelings. For instance, when asking questions about employment, ask what specific tasks clients enjoy and which they avoid. For example, they many avoid paperwork or accounting, while starting new projects may be a favorite activity. In addition, ask clients to rate the amount of attention needed in their work, and what type of job they would like if they could improve their concentration.

Cognitions or thinking patterns may reflect inattention or impulsivity. For example, information about whether adult clients see themselves as detail-oriented or organized can be important. This can be verified by asking about the status of their checkbook, neatness of their home or desk at work, or for the plot of a book, movie, or TV show they recently experienced (the amount of time spent in these activities is also a clue).

Decision making and social interactions can also demonstrate impulsivity. Ask client questions, such as:

- Do you take time to make decisions or jump into change?
- Are you an impulse buyer?
- Do you make decisions on the spot in response to sudden, strong emotions?
- Are you easily frustrated or angered?

Clients may report feelings of restlessness or irritability when subjected to quiet or sedentary activities without making actual signs of excessive movement. Information regarding frequency, intensity, and coping methods helps indicate the extent of the problem.

Barkley's interview may be modified for use with adults; especially if a parent accompanies the client. Although many questions can be answered by an adult reflecting on their childhood, memory is less reliable over time. Some DSM-IV criteria do not apply to adults (i.e., Oppositional Defiant or Conduct Disorders); other criteria do (i.e., Anxiety, Depression, and thought disorders). Adult disorders, such as personality disorders, can be added or substituted.

Observation Techniques

Observing clients in a natural setting (e.g., the classroom, a seminar or meeting, a work setting) can greatly enhance diagnosis. Clinicians can assess overactivity, inattention, impulsivity, and compliance with instructions in their own office; however, new stimuli and the clinician's one-on-one attention may suppress normal behaviors.

Begin observing clients from the moment they enter the waiting room, office, or any other setting. In the office, pay attention to signs of:

- **Motor restlessness**—Do clients fidget, tap their fingers or feet, or explore the room?

- **Attention and impulsivity**—What are clients' responses to being asked to wait, asked long and "boring" questions, or filling out forms and question-naires?

- **Social and relational skills**—How do clients interact with significant others that accompany them, and how do they relate to the therapist or examiner.[7] (This is especially important with adult clients, since other types of observation may not be practical.)

Observing Child Clients—Structured observation, used most frequently with children, allows the therapist to compare symptoms with same-aged peers as well as note situational variables, such as what tasks the child performs and the type and frequency of reinforcement they receive.[24]

One method of structured observation for children involves recording a child's different classroom behaviors (e.g., out of seat, off-task, or talking out of turn) during 10- or 30-second intervals. Observation periods may alternate between the child and several same-sex peers. This method allows direct symptom comparison with a "normal" peer group for diagno-sis, or the ongoing evaluation of behavior changes due to treatment.

A more structured observation method involves using the Child Behavior Checklist-Direct Observation Form (CBCL-DOF). This standardized measure gives the therapist: [25]

- Scores for mean time on tasks, total problems, and symptoms of behavioral mood disturbance
- Normative data
- A way to assess a broad spectrum of symptoms

Although structured observation techniques seem promising, there have been conflicting reports of how well the results correlate with ratings obtained from parents and/or teachers.[24,26,27] The lack of adequate samples across situations or tasks could partially explain these mixed results. A recent review of several studies using observation concluded that these techniques are valuable when used in a structured manner, and in conjunction with interview and other methods. [28]

Observing Adolescent Clients—Observation is used less with adolescents than with children. Peer relations are very important for those in this age group, and observation may be *stigmatizing*. Adolescents are typically more aware of the observation, and *reactivity effects* may increase at this age. In addition, the differences in an adolescent's environment may make direct observation more difficult (e.g., classes are shorter, there are numerous classrooms and teachers, and some classes require more movement (i.e., shop or P.E.).

stigmatizing—a mark on one's reputation

reactivity effects—different behaviors caused by being watched

Observing Adult Clients—Clinicians have generally ignored observation techniques in their assessments of adults. This is due, in part, to the reduction of overt signs of inattention and hyperactivity that occur as an individual matures. In addition, problems can also arise when a clinician attempts to unobtrusively watch someone in the workplace (e.g., disruption of work flow, embarrassment or questions from coworkers, or possibly jeopardizing a client's work status). The client's type of job may be more active and not lend itself to structured, comparative observation; however, it is possible to observe and compare behavior during seminars, meetings, or college classes to gather such information. Current research has not demonstrated the value of using these measures with the adult populations.

Standardized Assessment Measures

There are various behavior rating scales used to assess ADHD. These scales are easy to administer, can be completed quickly, and quantify how the behavior deviates from norms for a particular age and gender. Questionnaires have been designed to elicit parent and teacher observations as well as obtain self-reports from children and adolescents. These can help clinicians conduct follow-up assessments of treatment efficacy in addition to initial diagnosis.

The following overview explains various assessment measures currently in use. Barkley's work provides a more complete description and review of these tools.[3] Available instruments are:

- Parent Ratings
- Teacher Ratings
- Self Ratings (child and adult)
- Neuropsychological Tests
- Family Functioning Tests

A comparative listing of these instruments and their use immediately follows this overview on page 32.

Parent Ratings

The most commonly used parent rating measures are the Conners Parent Rating Scale-Revised (CPRS-R) and the Child Behavior Check List (CBCL).[29,30]

The CPRS-R contains 48 items scored on a 4-point scale (0-3) ranging from "not at all" to "very much." Scores are rated on five scales including Conduct Problems, Learning Problems, Psychosomatic, Impulsive-Hyperactive, and Anxiety. The CPRS-R Hyperactivity Index, based on 10 items, successfully discriminates ADHD from non-ADHD groups. In addition, it can indicate responsiveness to treatment if used before and after a treatment program (e.g., medication and/or parent training interventions).[29]

The CBCL contains 138 items scored on two scales, Social Competence and Behavior Problems. Children with ADHD score high on several factors on the Behavior Problems scale including Hyperactive, Aggressive, and Delinquent. Recent research indicates that the Attention Problems scale is the best predictor.[30,2] The CBCL has also been shown to help discriminate ADHD from Conduct and Anxiety Disorders.[31]

Other parent rating measures used less frequently are:

- The ADHD Rating Scale, a rating of the 14 DSM-III-R factors[3]

- The Home Situations Questionnaire (HSQ) an evaluation of how often problem behaviors occur in different situations[32]

- The Home Situations Questionnaire-Revised (HSQ-R), a more specific measure of attention and concentration across different situations[3]

- The Revised Ontario Child Health Study (OCHS) scales (Boyle, et. al., 1993), a measurement for diagnosing several disorders based on the DSM-III-R criteria[33]

Teacher Ratings

To validate an ADHD diagnosis, the therapist should obtain ratings from other adults besides parents who observe the child's behavior in different settings. The most common questionnaires available assess teachers' observations. These include:

- Conners Teacher Rating Scales-Revised (CTRS-R)[29]
- Child Behavior Rating Scale-Teacher's Report Form (CBCL-TRF)[30]

The CTRS-R is similar to the CPRS-R and contains 28 items scored on scales of Conduct Problems, Hyperactivity, and Inattentive-Passive. The 10-item Hyperactivity Index can quickly screen clients for ADHD and measure responsiveness to treatment. The CTRS-R demonstrates adequate reliability with parent ratings.[29] Research has also found that teachers' expectations and practice effects do not appear to hinder the usefulness of the CTRS-R.[35]

Less-frequently used measures include the School Situations Questionnaire, ADHD Rating Scale (using teacher norms), and the ADD-H Comprehensive Teacher Rating Scale (ACTeRS).[3,34]

The CBCL-TRF successfully discriminates children with ADHD from other children and has significant correlations with observation, the CBCL, and CTRS.[3,30]

The CBCL-TRF is a 126-item questionnaire that consists of two scales, Adaptive Functioning and Behavior Problems. Subscales of the Behavior Problems scale include:

- Anxious
- Social Withdrawal
- Unpopular
- Self-Destructive
- Obsessive-Compulsive
- Inattentive
- Nervous-Overactive
- Aggressive

Assessment of adolescents may include ratings from several teachers. A cross-section of situations, including a class or teacher the student likes best, worst, and average will provide good comparison scores and information.

Self Ratings

There are few self-report measures used to assess ADHD. The most common are the CBCL's Youth Self-Report form (CBCL-YSR) and the Wender Utah Rating Scale (WURS).

The CBCL-YSR is used primarily as a screening tool for symptoms associated with ADHD as there is no definitive category for attentional or hyperactive problems within the instrument.

The CBCL-YSR was designed for children and adolescents 11 to 18 years of age.[36] Similar to the teacher and parent forms, scores are rated on Competence and Behavior Problems scales.

The Wender Utah Rating Scale (WURS) was developed for use in retrospective diagnosis of ADHD in adults.[37] This scale contains 61 items and allows adult clients to rate childhood behaviors as descriptive of them on a 5-point scale (0-4). Ratings range from "not at all or slightly" (0) to "very much" (4). The scale appears to discriminate between adults with ADHD versus a depressed or "normal" population.[38] Adults with Borderline Personality Disorder or Atypical Depression seem to score high on this test because these groups can have overlapping symptoms.

Other self-report inventories have been developed by several clinicians and researchers.[7] These inventories generally consist of a checklist of either DSM criteria or the Utah Criteria developed by Wender.[37] Questions probe childhood behaviors and current symptoms of inattention, hyperactivity, and impulsivity.

Self-report instruments can be used to rule out Depression, whose sufferers can sometimes present symptoms characteristic of ADHD. Instruments that assess Depression include:

- The Children's Depression Inventory[39]
- The Reynolds Adolescent Depression Scale[40]
- The Beck Depression Inventory - Adolescent (ages 13-15)[41]
- The Beck Depression Inventory (ages 16 to adult)[42]

Self-report inventories can also discriminate ADHD from various adult psychiatric disorders such as anxiety, paranoia, or personality disorders. These inventories include:

- The Symptom Checklist 90-Revised[43]
- The Structured Clinical Interview for DSM-III-R[44]

Using self-report inventories helps lend credibility to an ADHD diagnosis.

Neuropsychological Testing

Neuropsychological testing is a better assessment tool for determining the absence of ADHD than it is for verifying the diagnosis. Poor performance on these tests can either result from symptoms of ADHD or a variety of extraneous factors. For example, motivation and reinforcement for performance can be affected by the structure and novelty of the testing situation (e.g., a "clinical" or office setting) and the therapist's one-on-one attention. Depression, learning disabilities, or anxiety are other possible causes of impaired scores.

Neuropsychological testing generally focuses on sustained attention, impulsivity, and neuropsychological or frontal lobe functions.[3,22]

Average or above-average performance on these tests can be used to fairly reliably rule out ADHD. With increased acceptance of the theory that ADHD involves impairment of frontal lobe functioning, use of neuropsychological testing for diagnosis has become more and more popular. Through this popularity, recognition of adult ADHD has increased, and neuropsychological testing has been used some to help with diagnosis in this population. Since no research to date has addressed the validity of these tests with adults, it is unknown how useful they are.

Tests of sustained attention and impulsivity compare performance with overall functioning. Frequently used neurological tests include:

- The Continuous Performance Test (CPT)[45]

- The Freedom from Distractibility (FD) factor on the Wechsler Intelligence Scale for Children, third edition (WISC-III)[46]

- The Matching Familiar Figures Test (MFFT)[47]

Although the CPT is one of the more reliable tests for discriminating ADHD, no standardized administration methods or appropriate norms currently exist.

The Continuous Performance Test (CPT), one of the most widely used instruments for testing sustained attention, measures response to a certain stimulus when multiple stimuli are presented rapidly. Scores are based on numbers of:

- Correct responses
- Errors of omission (missing correct stimuli)
- Errors of commission (responding to alternative stimuli)

Theoretically, all three scoring factors measure sustained attention, while errors of commission also measure impulsivity.[2,3] One computerized version of the CPT is the Gordon Diagnostic System.[48] Although *reliable*, there has been considerable controversy over the *validity* of the test. Several recent studies question whether the tasks actually measure attentional deficits similar to those that impair daily functioning.[49,50]

reliable—the extent to which the test produces similar results when administered at different times

validity—the extent to which a test measures what it claims to measure

The FD factor of the WISC-III uses the scores on the Arithmetic, Digit Span, and Coding subtests to measure attention and distractibility in children. However, FD offers limited usefulness as an ADHD diagnostic tool because its scales are unable to pinpoint what causes a particular score.[2,3,51] For example, these scales also measure short-term memory, numeric ability, visual-spatial skills, and perceptual-motor speed.

The WAIS-R has a similar factor also used to determine the presence of ADHD. No research has been completed with an adult population, but similar problems exist with the WAIS-R because results may be due to a variety of causes.

The MFFT, originally designed to measure impulsivity, derives its scores from response time and total number of errors in matching pictures to a sample. Efficacy results for this test have been mixed; and success in discriminating ADHD from other disorders has been limited. In addition, the MFFT has not helped therapists substantiate changes that occur as a result of medication (based on changes in response time and number of errors).[3]

No current tests provide established validity or reliability for either diagnosing ADHD or measuring an individual's response to treatment. Research focus on test efficacy has increased, but the debate continues as to whether such tests measure actual deficits.[14,49] Investigation of other methods, such as the Wisconsin Card Sort Test, showed initial promise; however, researchers have been unable to replicate the original findings.[52] Additional tests currently being investigated include the following:

These instruments need continued research to determine their usefulness in assessing ADHD.

- Stroop Word-Color Association Test[53]
- Hand Movements Test (a subtest of the Kaufman Assessment Battery for Children)[54]
- A verbal fluency word-list test[55]

Family Functioning

Investigate family situational factors to determine areas where intervention may decrease problem behaviors. Take a psychosocial history (e.g., the status of marital, parent/child, and sibling relationships as well as communication styles.)[56,57] Families members (including a child who has been diagnosed with ADHD) generally exhibit a higher level of discord and pathology.[56] Assess these factors informally through an interview or by using standardized tests that measure the family environment or parenting stress, such as:

Although not directly related to the diagnosis of ADHD, consideration of family functioning is an important part of the assessment.

- The Family Environment Scale[58]
- The Family Assessment Device[59]
- The Life Stressors and Resources Inventory[60]
- The Brief Symptom Inventory[61]
- The Symptom Checklist 90-Revised (SCL-90R)[43]
- The Parenting Stress Index[62]

The matrix on the following page provides an at-a-glance look at the most widely used assessments for diagnosing ADHD.

The therapist should selectively use these assessment instruments (as well as those currently being designed and updated) to avoid cumbersome and time-consuming processes. Each test offers limited diagnostic assessment capability, and all tests are best used to support interview and observation results. Carefully choose a few measures to clarify diagnosis and guide treatment planning. For example, parent and teacher questionnaires (such as the CBCL or CRTS) are quick and reliable and can provide information for follow-up during the interview.

Other measures can be selected according to specific needs. For example:

- Neuropsychological tests may be helpful after an interview that indicates a history of neurological problems or learning disabilities.

- A therapist may want to use depression measures with clients having a family history of depression.

ADHD Assessment Tools

Parent Ratings	Teacher Ratings	Self Ratings	Neurological Testing	Family Function/ Parenting Stress Ratings
Conners Parent Rating Scale-Revised (CPRS-R)	Conners Teacher Rating Scale-Revised (CTRS-R)	Child Behavior Scale-Youth Self-Report Form (CBCL-YSR)	Continuous Performance Test (CPT)	Family Environment Scale
Child Behavior Checklist (CBCL)	Child Behavior Scale-Teacher's Report Form (CBCL-TRF)	Children's Depression Inventory	Freedom from Distractibility (FD) factor on the WISC-III	Family Assessment Device
ADHD Rating Scale		Reynolds Adolescent Depression Scale		Life Stressors and Resources Inventory
Home Situations Questionnaire (HSQ)	ACTeRS		Matching Familiar Figures Test (MFFT)	Brief Symptom Inventory
	ADHD Rating Scale	Beck Depression Inventory		
Home Situations Questionnaire-Revised (HSQ-R)	School Situation Questionnaire			Symptom Checklist 90-Revised (SCL-90R)
		Wender Utah Rating Scale (WURS) (adult)		
Revised Ontario Child Health Study (OCHS)				Parenting Stress Index

What Differentiates ADHD from Other Disorders?

Diagnosing ADHD can become complicated because other conditions result in behaviors similar to those typical of ADHD. These disorders either require different interventions or occur simultaneously with ADHD. There are nine disorders or symptom areas for which differentiation must be addressed; they are:

- Conduct Disorder/Oppositional Defiant Disorder/ Antisocial Personality Disorder
- Learning Disabilities
- Dysthymia and Depression
- Hypomania
- Bipolar Disorder
- Anxiety Disorders
- Borderline Personality Disorder
- Normal Variations in Attention, Activity Level, or Organization
- Other Possible Genetic Disorders

Conduct Disorder/Oppositional Defiant Disorder/ Antisocial Personality Disorder

Aggressive and antisocial behaviors typical of Conduct Disorder (CD), Oppositional Defiant Disorder (ODD), and Antisocial Personality Disorder (APD) overlap with behaviors characteristic of ADHD.

CD—In one study, 30 to 50 percent of those studied exhibited symptoms of both disorders.[8] People with CD characteristically perform more frequent and more severe acts of physical aggression and illegal acts than those with ADHD. Children and adolescents with CD exhibit more severe and persistent overt hostility than those with ADHD.[1] In addition, individuals with ADHD are more likely to have developmental and cognitive delays than those with CD.[3]

ODD—Those with ODD typically resist doing tasks because of an unwillingness to conform to others' demands, rather than as a result of inattention and impulsivity. This difference is especially clear when evaluating how those who suffer from each disorder respond to activities of interest to them. When intrigued, those with ADHD will complete tasks willingly unlike those with ODD.

APD—This disorder has been reportedly more prevalent in adults with ADHD; researchers estimate that adults with ADHD are about 10 times more likely to have APD.[14,7] These high rates of co-morbidity typically result from undiagnosed CD as well as the association of school failure and low work status with both ADHD and APD.[14,63] APD can be differentiated from ADHD by behaviors that reflect a disregard for others (e.g., breaking the law, financial irresponsibility, "conning" others for pleasure or profit, and a lack of remorse after hurting someone).

Learning Disabilities

Specific academic disabilities (such as reading, spelling, math, or language) are closely interwoven with ADHD.

Studies of how often clients experience both ADHD and learning disabilities vary significantly in results, ranging from chance to 30 percent.[8,64] Because individuals with ADHD usually show some academic difficulty and underachievement, clinicians must determine whether the client suffers from ADHD, a learning disability, or coexisting disorders. Making a differential diagnosis requires:

- Assessment of the degree of impairment and impact on academics
- Careful examination of the order in which symptoms appear

When a learning disorder is the primary problem, disruptive behavior patterns are seen as the clients' response to academic problems. These disruptive behaviors would probably increase with age as the negative experiences that trigger them increase.[1,7,64] On the other hand, disruptive behaviors and social problems typical of ADHD will be noticed early and remain consistent over time.

Dysthymia and Depression

The rate of overlap between depressive symptoms and those characteristic of ADHD are unknown; however, persistent and marked dysphoric mood must be present before a therapist can diagnose mood disorder.[1,7] Symptoms of inattention, irritability, and hyperactivity can result from depression, especially in children. Specific situations may account for some signs of low-level adjustment problems or depression; therefore, a recent history of these symptoms without accompanying developmental irregularities would indicate depression rather than ADHD.

Hypomania

ADHD and hypomania have many symptoms in common, such as irritability, rapid speech, disrupted sleep, and disorganization. Important differences relate to mood and insight. Individuals with hypomania will demonstrate inappropriate levels of *euphoria* or happiness and deny problems or symptoms. The overlap of Affective Disorders with ADHD is unknown; rates range from chance to over 70 percent, and there has been no consistency in results to date.[8]

euphoria—a sense of extreme elation and heightened activity

Bipolar Disorder

Those with Bipolar Disorder experience more cyclical mood disturbance and more intense hyperactivity and impulsivity than those with ADHD. Tantrums will be more extreme and last longer; destructiveness will be more purposeful than accidental. Symptoms of Bipolar Disorder in children are hard to differentiate from those of ADHD. The rate of Bipolar Disorder in children is unknown; however, it is most likely under-recognized and diagnosed.

Children with Bipolar Disorder will anticipate and relish fights rather than just "stumble into them." The client's biological disturbances will also be exacerbated with Bipolar Disorder (e.g., sleep is minimal and appetite may vary from nonexistent to binging.) In addition, perceptual disturbances such as *delusions* may occur.

Because evidence exists that there is a high rate of ADHD in adolescents with bipolar disorder, differential diagnosis is critical with this age group. Differentiating between ADHD and Bipolar Disorder in adolescents and adults relies on an analysis of symptom length and severity. Children with Bipolar Disorder usually do not experience concrete episodes

delusions- a belief that someone maintains despite much evidence to the contrary. For example, children may persist in believing that they are cartoon characters while adults may believe that they are superhuman.

of depression or mania; however, they may exhibit some of these symptoms in an erratic pattern. Adolescents and adults with Bipolar Disorder usually have more clearly defined instances of depression and mania such as sleep disturbance, sudden onset, or delusional symptoms.[65]

Anxiety Disorders

In a treatment setting, individuals with coexisting ADHD and anxiety disorders are less likely to respond to stimulant medication such as Ritalin.[8]

Researchers estimate that there is a 25 percent overlap between ADHD and anxiety disorders (e.g., overanxious disorder, phobic disorders, and generalized anxiety disorder).[8] Common symptoms of anxiety disorders, such as restlessness, irritability, impatience, and sleep disturbance are similar to those experienced with ADHD; however, signs of impulsivity are not reported with anxiety disorders. In addition, anxiety disorder symptoms are generally of shorter duration, are accompanied by signs of autonomic nervous system arousal (e.g., sweaty palms, heart palpitations, dizziness, and frequent urination), and include rumination about the future or potential misfortune.[1]

Borderline Personality Disorder (BPD)

There are important differences between BPD and ADHD even though impulsivity, substance abuse, and impaired relationships are common to both disorders. While adult relationships for those with ADHD are often impaired or unsuccessful, they are not characterized by intense, wildly fluctuating emotions. With BPD, suicide and self-mutilation are more common, and the symptoms of hyperactivity and inattention are not marked.[1,7]

Normal Variations in Attention, Activity Level, or Organization

Many people experience a decreased tolerance for sitting still, listening, or paying attention to detail. The important difference between these people and those with ADHD is the level of impairment in daily functioning and longevity of the symptoms. For instance, a "squirmy" child who constantly moves in their seat may be able to concentrate and get good grades, or an adult under stress at home may temporarily be forgetful and disorganized at work.

Other Possible Genetic Disorders

There are several genetic disorders characterized by typical ADHD symptoms of inattention and hyperactivity. These include:

- *Turner syndrome in females*—A disorder resulting from a missing sex chromosome that is marked by a lack of primary reproductive organs and secondary sexual characteristics (body hair, body shape, voice tone, and short stature).

- *XYY syndrome in males*—A chromosomal abnormality in which there is the presence of a third chromosome associated with low fertility.

- *Fragile X syndrome*—Primarily a male disorder of dysfunctional development on the X chromosome. Atypical physical features include a long face and large head and ears. Behavioral characteristics include cluttered speech, hyperactivity, autism, and meaningless, repetitive hand movements.

- *Neurofibromatosis*—A familial condition afflicting children, characterized by developmental changes in the nervous system, muscles, bones, and skin marked by tumors over the body in pigmented areas.[64]

- *Early treated Phenylketonuria (PKU)*—A missing enzyme that results in severe and permanent mental retardation if untreated.[63]

- *Pervasive Developmental Disorders (PDD)*—Serious and pervasive dysfunctions of basic psychological functioning in social, cognitive, perceptual, attentional, motor, and/or linguistic functions.

- *Autistic Disorder*—A type of PDD marked by the withdrawal from reality into oneself; a tendency to be absorbed in one's thought and fantasies.

- *Fetal Alcohol Syndrome*—Abnormal anatomical features and psychological deficits including growth deficiencies, skeletal malformations, mental retardation, hyperactivity, and heart murmurs resulting from severe maternal alcoholism during pregnancy.

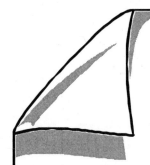

*Therapy Notes from
the Desk of Pat Owen*

*Completed assessment on T.J. He has Low Average intelligence
from WISC-III scores, a learning disability in reading, and ex-
pressive language. Reports from mother and T.J. are of poor
attention/concentration, high impulsivity, and hyperactivity
since a very young age (approximately age 2). Mother reports
him being a fussy baby who cried a great deal and was hard to
feed. Current teacher and history of report cards indicate
similar long-standing problems. Fighting at school started 3
years ago and has escalated recently. No other history of
conduct disorder. Fighting might be a response to frustrations
experienced with school work. Maternal risk factors include
difficult birth (breech baby), maternal smoking, and moderate
drinking during pregnancy. Mother has brother who had ADHD-
type problems, but was never diagnosed. Father has familial
history of mental retardation (sister). Mother and Father
divorced six years ago with some continued stress in that
relationship. Medical history and current physical work up not
significant for any disorders. Diagnosis ADHD. Recommend trial
of stimulant mediation and psychotherapy.*

Chapter Three: Treating the Disorder

Diary of Todd J.

May 27

Things seem to be going better. My grades are better at school, and it's a little easier to pay attention. Mom thinks it's because of the pills, but I don't know. The doctor wants me to keep taking them even though I won't be seeing her anymore. She helped me not get so mad so fast; now I don't fight with my friends so much. I've been on this reward program at home which isn't too bad. I get points for finishing my homework and doing stuff like taking out the trash. I can trade in my points for money and time to play video games at the mall. Things are way better, both at school and at home!

This chapter answers the following:

What are the Major Issues in Treating ADHD?— This section explains how the lack of consistent research regarding etiology affects difficulties in ADHD treatment.

What Biological Factors May Cause ADHD?— This section examines the genetic, neurologic, and predisposing factors that may cause ADHD.

How Can ADHD be Treated With Medication?— This section discusses the use of stimulants, antidepressants, and antihypertensive medications to treat ADHD.

What are the Environmental Influences that May Cause ADHD?— This section describes how substances in a person's environment as well as familial relationships may affect ADHD.

What are the Major Issues in Treating ADHD?

Developing effective treatment methods for any disorder requires an ability to determine what causes the disorder. Although many factors have been linked to ADHD, how they are linked is still uncertain. There is clearly a genetic component in a substantial percentage of individuals; however, those with no known predisposition show signs of ADHD. Factors in the client's physical environment (such as toxins) or in their primary relationships (such as family dysfunction) can provide partial explanations.

Both environmental and biological causes implicate frontal lobe functioning in some manner, either structurally, biochemically, or a combination of both. There has been some *longitudinal research—* research on the same people conducted over a period of several years.

prognoses— outcome in the future

For a more comprehensive discussion of ADHD etiology, see Barkley or Lorys-Vernon, Hynd, Lyytinen, & Hern.[3,9]

genetic— chromosomes that influence the development of an organism

heritability— the percentage of transmissions of chromosomal links, from one generation to another

polygenetic— multiple genes involved in the disorder

consistency of research results on genetic links and associations between frontal lobe damage and ADHD symptoms.[65,9] Further research is needed to assess each of these causes in detail, especially intensive *longitudinal research.*

On a positive note, evidence exists that there are subtypes of ADHD. These subtypes reflect a different basic cause or etiology, have different symptom pictures, and require different treatment responses.[16] ADHD may turn out to be a prominent label for a number of disorder subtypes with distinctive causes that respond to different treatments and show varied *prognoses.*

Theories of ADHD etiology originally focused on brain damage, using evidence from neurological soft signs such as minor physical anomalies, rather than results from objective data or test results. When results were contradictory, researchers began to focus on genetic or environmental factors. Again, only partial support for environmental causes has been found. Current theories lean towards an interaction between biological and environmental factors. Interventions based on behavioral reinforcement combined with stimulant medications have proven most effective to date. However, no theory (even an integrated viewpoint) yet adequately explains all instances of ADHD. Each subtype must be examined to determine possible causes and treatment strategies.

This chapter briefly describes the most common theories related to biological and environmental factors that may cause ADHD and treatment methods that support each theory.

What Biological Factors May Cause ADHD?

Biologic factors that have been linked to ADHD include:

- *Genetic/Heritability* Factors
- Neurological Factors
- Predisposing Factors

Genetic/Heritability Factors

Based on the fact that most research evidence points to *polygenetic* transmission patterns, a definite genetic component exists with ADHD. Some genetic support comes from recent evidence showing a link between ADHD and Generalized Resistance to Thyroid Hormone (RTH), a genetic condition with a high heritability factor. This condition has been closely associated with symptoms of ADHD and not with other forms of behavior or psychiatric disorders.[17] Although this research is promising for ADHD assessment and detection, RTH accounts for only a small percentage of those diagnosed with ADHD and may eventually be considered a subtype of the disorder.

Further genetic support comes from family and twin studies which generally reflect some degree of heritability of ADHD. Heritability rates differ in the studies, and it is still unclear as to what traits specifically are inherited.[8,64] Substantial evidence indicates as high as a 50 percent rate of familial transmission of factors such as temperament, activity level, and shyness, all of which could impact the manifestation of ADHD.[9,64]

Research has also demonstrated a link between children with ADHD and increased levels of psychiatric disorder in their parents. This could indicate support for a polygenetic transmission, with parents contributing components of the disorder, or more direct transmission if parents had been misdiagnosed and actually have ADHD. This link might also indicate the consequences of a chaotic family life. The results of several adoption studies however, uphold theories of genetic transmission of ADHD components rather than environmental causes.[64]

Though several studies have investigated familial (genetic) transmission of ADHD directly, results have been contradictory. This is partially due to an overlap of ADHD symptoms and aggression. More recent studies have factored out aggressive behavior in the research analysis and still generally found moderate levels of heritability of ADHD.[8]

Neurological Factors

Neurologic dysfunction, the basis of ADHD's original conceptualization, has been increasingly targeted for study. As more sophisticated equipment has been developed, there has been a corresponding increase in speculation regarding the role of ADHD in frontal lobe functioning, *biochemical agents,* and brain structure.[9,64] Regardless of the research methodology used, the frontal lobe appears to be prominently

Theories regarding a link between brain functioning and ADHD have recently increased in popularity.

biochemical agents—
neurotransmitters or chemicals in the brain that affect behavior as well as mood and thought processes

and consistently involved in ADHD, either as a result of structural or biochemical differences.

Pennington has postulated that an analysis of frontal lobe functioning is very important for understanding the impact of ADHD.

Frontal lobe functioning—Results of studies based on theories of brain activity have been mixed. Cortical overarousal (excessive brain activity), is a popular idea that has been refuted after numerous studies. However, there is some evidence that brain underactivity may result from a decreased blood flow to the frontal lobes which could interfere with alertness and other brain functioning.[9,64]

Frontal lobe analysis is also crucial for understanding the variability and general decrease (over time) in levels of hyperactivity among those with ADHD. Frontal lobe damage effects many symptom behaviors, especially disorganization, distractibility, and impulsivity. Pennington explains that *executive functions* operate in the frontal and prefrontal areas of the brain. These areas act as control systems that coordinate multiple brain operations and include planning, selective attention, inhibition, and initiation of cognitions and social behaviors. Structural or biochemical damage to the frontal lobe could result in many ADHD-like changes in behaviors related to executive functions.[64]

executive functions— brain activity involved in the organization and integration of various brain functions

dopamine, serotonin, and norepinepherine—chemicals in the brain that help regulate motor-control systems and central nervous system functioning

Biochemical agents—Although theories on the role of biochemical agents (e.g., *dopamine, serotonin, and norepinephrine)* have abounded, effective research has been limited with inconclusive results. These theories have been based on animal studies. They rely on associations made between how stimulants increase levels of dopamine and norepinephrine in animals, with how those stimulants could be effective in treating ADHD in humans. No direct evidence of a link has been demonstrated in human subjects to date. Some evidence indicates that serotonin might play a role in ADHD because animals have shown increased aggression and hyperactivity when serotonin levels were depleted. However, studies of hyperactive humans have not consistently upheld this hypothesis. The most promising theory published emphasizes the relationship between ADHD behaviors and a combined action of biochemical agents including dopamine, norepinephrine, and serotonin depletion related to ADHD behaviors.[9,64]

CT scan technology— computerized x-ray of the brain

Brain Structure—Preliminary studies using *CT scan technology* failed to show any differences in the brains of children with ADHD from those of "normals," but questions regarding poor diagnostic clarity and CT technology limited the usefulness of results.[9] Further studies using *MRI* scans use more stringent diagnostic criteria and appear more reliable. These results do not indicate the presence of brain damage; however, significant size differences in various structures including the frontal lobe and ventricular horn were consistent for subjects with ADHD. More research will be necessary to find a pattern of differences in those with ADHD and determine the relationship between these differences and behavioral symptoms.[9]

MRI— Magnetic Resonance Imaging, a radiological process for taking pictures of internal structures

For more detailed information regarding neurologic factors that contribute to ADHD, see Lorys-Vernon, Hynd, Lyytinen, & Hern and Pennington.[9,64]

Predisposing Factors

Those factors that may predispose a child to ADHD include:

- Prenatal and postnatal difficulties
- Maternal substance abuse

Prenatal and postnatal difficulties–Excessive fetal activity, inadequate health care, birth trauma, early neurologic damage, and low birth weight may increase the risk of ADHD. However, most information on these factors is retrospective and anecdotal, with no clear evidence that such events predict ADHD.[3,8]

Maternal substance abuse–High levels of maternal alcohol abuse during pregnancy may cause *Fetal Alcohol Syndrome*, which presents a symptom picture with many similarities to ADHD. Although no clear link with ADHD has been established, lower levels of alcohol abuse or abuse of other types of substances may also have *intrauterine* effects and result in learning disabilities, *disinhibition*, and disruptive behaviors.[8,64] Other substance-related behaviors associated with risk are:

Fetal Alcohol Syndrome— abnormal anatomical features and psychological deficits including growth deficiencies, skeletal malformations, mental retardation, hyperactivity, and heart murmurs

- Cigarette smoking during pregnancy

- Maternal caffeine use during pregnancy

intrauterine— inside the uterus

- Use of other substances during pregnancy (e.g., prescription medications, antibiotics, and sleeping pills)

disinhibition— the lowering of inhibitions that results in behaviors occurring spontaneously, without thought

How Can ADHD be Treated with Medication?

Medications used to treat ADHD target symptoms of inattention, impulsivity, hyperactivity, mild aggression, and non-compliance. Although these medications are used to treat ADHD symptoms, they do not cure the disorder.

Those concerned with using medications to treat ADHD point out that abuse of illegal drugs might result from regular use of stimulant medication. However, no evidence exists that the use of stimulant medication to control ADHD symptoms leads to other types of drug use or misuse.[3,5,66]

Commonly Prescribed Medications

Medications commonly prescribed for those diagnosed with ADHD include:

- Stimulants

- Tricyclic antidepressants

- Anti-hypertensive agents (occasionally prescribed, usually in combination with one of the other two types)

Stimulants

Stimulants, which are medications that increase the arousal of the Central Nervous System, appear effective in treating ADHD across all ages, from early childhood through adulthood.[21] The most frequently used medication for treating ADHD is methylphenidate (MPH), popularly known as Ritalin. This stimulant medication has received the greatest attention and use; other commonly used types include dextroamphetamine (Dexedrine) and pemoline (Cylert). Often alternate medications need to be tried after an initial failure of a single type.[66]

On the surface, it seems odd to treat a disorder marked by hyperactive and impulsive symptoms with a stimulant medication; however, stimulants appear to reduce symptoms by:

- Increasing the release of certain neurotransmitters, namely dopamine and norepinephrine, into the area (synapse) between the nerve cells in the brain

- Blocking the re-absorption of these same neurotransmitters back into the nerve cell that released them

Researchers have been unable to clarify exactly what area of the brain is most important for the effect of the stimulants on ADHD, but the frontal cortex and the striatum are likely involved.

Dosage—MPH and most stimulant medications are effective for a short period of time, which necessitates a morning and noon dose for the adult or child. Typical dosage ranges from 5-30 mg./day, but may start at 2.5 mg. for children under six.[67] The dosage for dextroamphetamine is one-half that of methylphenidate. Some forms of time-release capsules are available to reduce administration frequency to once a day; however, capsules should not be taken in the evening as they may disrupt sleep.

Researchers have found that the amount of medication needed is fairly consistent across age groups rather than being dependent on age or size.[7]

Side Effects—Side effects of stimulants may include disrupted appetite and sleep patterns, headaches, and stomach aches. Less common side effects (but potentially more problematic) are motor and/or vocal tics and some inhibition of growth. Many of these effects are short-term and can be managed by adjusting dosage or not taking the drug during weekends or vacations (drug "holidays").[3,66] Clients tend to tolerate these medications well, and the clinician can switch to another stimulant if side effects occur.[67]

Antidepressants

Other medications used to treat ADHD consist mainly of various tricyclic antidepressants, such as fluoxetine, nortriptyline, and desipramine.[68,69,70] Results indicate some level of effectiveness, especially when these antidepressants are used in conjunction with stimulant medication. Major benefits include improved mood and decreased hyperactivity, and these medications appear useful for all ages.[8,70]

Combined use of antidepressants and stimulants requires close monitoring to prevent toxicity since MPH interferes with metabolism of the tricyclics.[67]

In general, the best types of antidepressants to use are those without mood-elevating properties, such as nortryptiline, desipramine, or certraline.

Dosage—Dosage ranges are typically 20 to 80 mg./day. These medications need to be used with caution in children less than 12 years of age. Additionally, the use of these medications in conjunction with a stimulant medication elevates the levels of both drugs. The effects of antidepressant medication on ADHD, either alone or in conjunction with stimulants, have not been studied extensively in adults.[71]

Side Effects—A common side effect of antidepressant use is drowsiness, but this usually subsides over time. Additional side effects include dry mouth, decreased appetite, headaches, and insomnia.

Anti-hypertensive Agents

Clonidine has demonstrated some effectiveness in children with tics and extreme levels of activity, impulsivity, and aggression. Although not used exclusively, this medication may be used in conjunction with other medications for certain clients.

Dosage—Typical dosages are from .1 to .3 mg./day. The safety of this drug has not been established for children below 12 years of age.

Side Effects— Common side effects include nausea, vomiting, sedation, headaches, and dizziness.

Effectiveness of Medications for Treating ADHD

Although some improvement in family and peer relationships has been noted with the use of medication, research generally indicates continued impairment in the way the person with ADHD functions. Their ratings remain below those expected at normal levels of functioning.[66]

Efficacy in Children—Research supports the practice of giving stimulant medication to children to increase their compliance, sustained attention, and organization while decreasing impulsivity. These research results reflect success with 60 to 90 percent of the children studied.[8] Two areas where efficacy becomes questionable are the effects on family and peer relationships as well as the effects on very young children.

Medication seems to be less effective with preschool-age children. Some research shows that although the medication may decrease hyperactive and inattentive behaviors, side effects (including appetite and sleep disturbance, as well as clinging behavior) outweigh any benefits.[7] Based on these results, medication for very young children should be used cautiously.

Efficacy in Adolescents—Adolescents appear to respond similarly to children with regard to effects of medication; however, the magnitude of the change may not be as great. Although researchers have been able to demonstrate short-term improvements, long-term effects remain less understood. There is some evidence that although classroom behavior improves, overall school achievement does not.[72]

Efficacy in Adults—Few studies have systematically examined how well medication works with adults. Those that have, discovered similar rates of success as experienced with children.[71,74]

Conclusions regarding long-term use are not definitive because of the limited quantity and methodology of existing studies. Because children diagnosed with ADHD often continue to exhibit social or other problems, future research needs to address the long-term effectiveness of medications.

For an in-depth review of the effectiveness of stimulant medication in treating ADHD, see Barkley or Weiss & Hechtman.[3,7]

Some researchers have noted a decrease in the effects of medication during the second year of treatment for all age groups.[73] Although improvements in relationships have been noticed at the beginning of drug treatment, this effect tends to fade over time.[67]

A few studies have indicated some long-term effectiveness for using medications to control inattention and hyperactivity.

What are the Environmental Influences that May Cause ADHD?

Many theorists believe that either the substances found in a person's environment or interpersonal relationships in home and school settings play a major role in the origin of ADHD. This section examines the following:

- ***Substances in the Physical Environment***—These include lead, food additives, food allergies, caffeine, and sugar.

- ***Developmental Causes***—These theories consider the interplay between personality, biology, and environmental pressures that affect ADHD.

- ***Cognitive-Behavioral Approaches***—These approaches focus on thought processes that affect behavior and use reinforcement principles to change behavior.

Substances in the Physical Environment that May Cause ADHD

In the search for definitive clues as to the origin of ADHD, some researchers have studied how elements present in a person's physical environment may be potential causes of ADHD. Certain substances (e.g., lead or various foods) can become toxic when ingested or produce an allergic reaction. Research to date has targeted the effects of lead, nutrition, caffeine, sugar, and food allergies on people's environments. However, results have shown no definitive, verifiable links between these and ADHD.

Lead

Researchers have long believed that exposure to lead, even at low levels, can cause ADHD. Recent studies have revealed a small, but reliable, link between decreased academic performance and increased distractibility and impulsivity for children exposed to lead. These effects appear to last into adolescence and impact cognitive and behavioral performance in a manner typical of ADHD.[75,8]

Food Additives

The debate regarding food additives became viable again when a recent study by Boris and Mandel found that 19 of 26 ADHD subjects reacted positively (e.g., behavior and attention improved) in response to a multiple-item-elimination diet.[78]

During the 1970s, a widely reported study alleged food additives, preservatives, and salicylates led to hyperactivity in a large number of children. The study attempted to control behavior by eliminating these substances from children's diets.[76] While this study sparked huge interest, these findings could not be replicated in many subsequent controlled studies. In addition, these controlled studies could not substantiate the notion that removing food additives from a person's diet can control or decrease hyperactivity.[9,77]

Food Allergies

Rather than a primary cause of ADHD, food intolerance or other allergies may exacerbate behavior in some cases.

Allergic reactions to several foods (e.g., aspartame, milk, eggs, and peanuts) may cause ADHD symptoms. Most information on these foods has been anecdotal, with few empirical studies completed. One recent study failed to find an association between a number of allergic symptoms and ADHD.[79] Generally, dietary treatments are only effective when a direct causal relationship exists between a specific food and a specific child.

Caffeine

Research on caffeine intake as a cause of ADHD has produced no solid causative link. However, significant research has addressed the use of caffeine as a treatment for the disorder. While caffeine sometimes proves effective in decreasing hyperactivity symptoms, the evidence has primarily shown minimal or negative results. Caffeine appears inferior to stimulant medications for treating ADHD.[77]

Sugar

For some time, the public has believed that sugar intake causes hyperactivity in children. Both parents and teachers commonly report increased activity level, impulsivity, irritability, and shortened attention span after children ingest sugar. However, when several controlled studies examined this theory, the overwhelming results suggested no appreciable behavior, cognitive, or mood changes related to ingesting sugar.[3,77]

Despite research results to the contrary, many continue to believe that sugar intake causes hyperactivity in children.

Developmental Theories that Address the Origin and Treatment of ADHD

Many theories regarding familial impact result from social learning, family systems, and developmental approaches to the origins and treatment of mental disorders. Regardless of etiology, this section will help clarify the family's role in ADHD therapy.

Relationships and family interactions can play a significant role in ADHD.

Developmental theorists point to early sleep and feeding practices as reflective of the interplay between personality, biology, and environmental pressures that can affect ADHD. Sleep disturbances are not uncommon for children. Some infants can be excessively drowsy and unresponsive, while others sleep poorly due to overreactivity and restlessness. Feeding difficulties can include irregular appetites, "picky eating," poor sucking, or crying that interferes with nutritional intake.

Early sleep and feeding patterns contribute to family difficulties that, in turn, increase the chances of ADHD.

Parents dealing with these difficulties must devote excessive time and may become very frustrated trying to soothe the infant or complete basic caretaking tasks. This situation could interfere with the child's emotional and cognitive

mirroring and imitation—
verbal and nonverbal
mimicking of facial expres-
sions, movements, or
vocalizations

development by limiting the time parents have for positive interactive play with their children, such as *mirroring and imitation* that increase smiling, vocalizaitions, and cuddling. Parents dealing with such frustrations experience feelings of incompetence, anger, guilt, and helplessness that the child may sense and respond to by becoming increasingly agitated, irritated, impulsive, and inattentive.

This type of interplay impacts an infant's personality development. Both Attachment Theory and Erickson's Stage Theory address this impact.

Attachment Theory

Attachment theory promotes the idea that the caregiver's and the baby's temperaments influence the degree and quality of their attachment to one another. For instance, when an excitable, timid adult tries to deal with a demanding, difficult infant, fewer positive interactions may result and emotional ties between the two may be inhibited.[80] A lack of positive emotion (attachment) between an infant and caregiver makes learning cognitive skills and social development (bonding with others) more difficult. Such a lack of attachment may lead to behavior problems related to violating social norms or expectations of authority figures later in life, some of which are characteristic of ADHD (e.g., not listening when spoken to directly, not following instructions, or breaking rules).

Erickson's Stage Theory

This approach emphasizes various stages of psychosocial development and addresses the consequences of inadequate parent-child interactions. This theory proposes that the success of mastering a developmental stage, or task, depends on the success of previous task completion.

Erickson's developmental stages are:

1. **Trust vs. mistrust** (ages 0-1)—basic needs are met reliably

2. **Autonomy vs. shame and doubt** (ages 1-3)— striving to learn independence and self confidence

3. **Initiative vs. guilt** (ages 3-5)—learning to initiate tasks, learning self control

4. *Competence vs. inferiority* (ages 6-12)—developing physical, *cognitive*, and social skills to feel effective

5. *Identity vs. role confusion* (ages 12-19)—trying out roles and forming an integrated identity

6. *Intimacy vs. isolation* (ages 20-40)—forming close lasting relationships and making career commitments

7. *Generativity vs. stagnation* (ages 40-65)—contributing to the world through family and creative, productive work

8. *Integrity vs. despair* (ages 65+)—thinking back on life with either satisfaction or disappointment

The following addresses how certain stages appear to significantly impact those with ADHD.

Stage One—The first and most basic task for an infant to master is trust.[19] For example, when parents are unable to meet infant needs for stimulation or affection, infants learn to mistrust their environment and people within that environment. Once this mistrust exists, other tasks (e.g., completing school, forming an identity, and learning to get along with others) become more difficult.

Stage Two—The inability to trust will generally result in subsequent delays in mastering developmental tasks. These delays typically involve children's ability to learn "*autonomy*" rather than learning "shame, doubt, and guilt."[19] For instance, toilet training is a typical task thought to encourage autonomy and initiative. Distractibility and inattention may make learning that task more difficult. In addition, parents who feel overwhelmed with toilet training may give the child more attention (usually negative) for not learning the task.

Stage Five—Early delays in development can have a significant impact into adolescence. According to Erickson, the psychosocial stage for adolescence involves a conflict labelled, "identity vs. role confusion."[19] Resolving this conflict requires testing numerous roles and integrating them into a cohesive sense of self. Success depends on both the adolescent's ability to master this task and successful resolution of previous stages. Generally, adolescents with ADHD

cognitive— *thinking abilities*

autonomy— *a sense of independence*

For the child as well as the parents, feelings of shame and guilt may accompany the child's failure to use bathrooms appropriately in public.

have been unsuccessful with previous tasks and have often failed to fit into roles expected by society (e.g., being a "good student" or a "respectful son"). Although clinical ADHD symptoms decrease as the child becomes an adolescent, the individual continues to have social and academic problems due to these previous developmental delays.

Stages Six and Seven—Psychosocial delays throughout a person's childhood and adolescence continue to impact them as adults. Problematic tasks involve attempting to form close, lasting relationships and making commitments (intimacy vs. isolation) as well as making contributions to the world through work, family, and creativity (generativity vs. stagnation). An adult with ADHD typically has a pattern of unstable relationships, making intimacy more difficult. Repeated failures at work may also hinder successful resolution of these stages.

Developmental Treatment Methods

Developmental treatment methods involve traditional individual psychotherapy and family therapy.

Individual therapy may be indicated if there are coexisting signs of depression or anxiety, or if certain situational stressors or trauma exist. In these cases, therapists should take an active role and structure sessions to increase the client's interest.[3]

Individual Psychotherapy—Individual psychotherapy is not the treatment of choice for children diagnosed with ADHD. Some evidence indicates that the reason psychotherapy may be ineffective is that the inattention and overactivity characteristic of ADHD preclude client insight or their ability to clarify inner thoughts and feelings.[7]

Adults may benefit from certain types of individual therapy, emphasizing cognitive and behavioral changes to manage their disorder.

Family systems theorists focus on the roles people establish within their family. A child with ADHD may take on the role of "clown" or "troublemaker," thus perpetuating disruptive behaviors and chaotic relationships.

Family Therapy—Family therapy can be used effectively either to help implement targeted behavioral interventions or to assist family members experiencing difficulties that may hinder the therapy process. For example, many families who have children with ADHD deal with personal distress, depression, or other significant stressors including their child's chronic disability. Under these stressful situations, family members divert energy away from general parenting responsibilities at the same time that the family must assume additional responsibilities for coping with ADHD.

Conducted by experienced family therapists, traditional family therapy is best for facilitating ADHD therapy by helping parents or other family members stabilize the home environment.

Effectiveness of Individual Psychotherapy and Family Therapy

A recent review of ADHD treatment methods suggests that traditional psychotherapy, particularly psychoanalysis, is ineffective for treating children with ADHD.[81] Family therapy may be indicated if there are coexisting signs of depression, anxiety, or other difficulties.

The most successful family psychotherapy programs have combined more traditional therapy with psychoeducational techniques such as parent training and problem solving, with frequent practice and skill rehearsal. These programs use similar techniques as individual treatment, but expand the focus of treatment from the child to the family unit. Barkley has developed an extensive program utilizing cognitive-behavioral techniques combined with a family systems approach. His program includes family and parent sessions as well as a children's group.[3]

In general, family therapy is inadequate when used as the sole ADHD treatment approach. It is most effective when combined with psychoeducational techniques such as parent training and problem-solving skills training.

For detailed descriptions of parent training and problem-solving strategies, see pages 57 through 60 as well as page 64

Cognitive-Behavioral Theories that Address the Origin and Treatment of ADHD

This section reviews behavioral theories and cognitive-behavioral approaches including treatment strategies and efficacy. Behavior therapy relies on principles of *reinforcement.* Cognitive theories are based on altering the thought processes that affect behavior. Currently, clinicians use both behavioral and cognitive techniques in therapy because of the interplay between cognitions (thoughts) and behavior. This form of treatment is labelled "cognitive-behavioral."

reinforcement—any consequence that increases the frequency of the preceding behavior

Behavioral Theory

Behavioral theory is based on the belief that learning new behaviors depends on the response that follows. Behavior principles state that a behavior or the frequency of a behavior can be changed by a consequence or a reinforcer. For change to occur, the reinforcers must be important to the individual

Most behavioral therapy programs include strategies, such as:

- *Positive reinforcement*

- *Time out*

- *Development of specific goals and consequences for identified positive and negative behaviors*

whose behavior is being modified. For example, attention may be highly valued by one child, while earning television or phone time may be a more effective reinforcer for another child. These principles include positive and negative reinforcement, punishment, time out, and extinction.

Positive Reinforcement—This type of reinforcement occurs when consequences that follow behaviors increase behaviors and reflect something added to the situation. For example, if a child sitting quietly in a chair received praise from a parent, and the child liked the praise and consequently sat quietly more often, then sitting quietly was positively reinforced by the praise. Similarly, if a child is screaming and the parents' attention to the screaming behavior (by commenting or yelling) increases their screams, then positive reinforcement has also occurred.

Negative Reinforcement—This reinforcement also increases behavior, but the consequence reflects something taken away whose absence is viewed as a positive consequence. The removal of this reinforcement increases the behavior. For example, if a child's parents stop fighting when the child breaks a lamp, then the parental fights may become negative reinforcement, resulting in an increase in the child's destructive behavior.

Punishment—This approach differs from negative reinforcement in that something is taken away whose absence is viewed as a negative consequence. This removal decreases behavior frequency. For example, phone privileges may be taken away from a teenager if they come home late. If either the frequency or degree of late arrivals decreases, loss of phone privileges function as an effective punishment.

Time Out—This approach removes a child from a reinforcing environment. The child is removed to another, less stimulating environment for a designated period of time. A common example of this is children sitting on a kitchen chair or being sent to their room. Although time out is intended only to change the stimuli in the environment, children generally view it as a punishment.

Generally, extinction works best when combined with positive reinforcement for a new behavior to replace the old one.

Extinction—Like punishment, extinction decreases behavior. It is a process of ignoring a behavior until it stops completely. For example, when parents ignore a child's temper tantrum, and the tantrum eventually stops, the likelihood decreases that the child will have a tantrum in the future. However, before the behavior tapers off and eventually decreases, there is usually a "response burst" (or dramatic increase in the behavior) for a short period of time.

Behavioral Treatments

Treatment methods that utilize a behavioral reinforcement system are based on the behavior principles reviewed above. These reinforcement programs can also be used in public or in the classroom. Implementing such a system in the home requires:

Most behavior programs train parents and teachers to alter consequences in order to increase adaptive, on-task behaviors and minimize intrusive, disruptive behaviors.

1. Identifying target behaviors (e.g., increase homework; increase chore completion; raise hand before speaking).

2. Determining the reinforcement frequency necessary for behavioral change (e.g., daily, hourly, each chore given).

3. Pinpointing appropriate reinforcers (e.g., fifteen minutes of 1:1 attention with a parent each night; earn a point toward receiving a special toy).

4. Explaining the program to the child and beginning reinforcement.

5. Being consistent.

6. Evaluating effectiveness on an ongoing basis. Conduct periodic reviews to determine when a goal has been reached, what new goals can be added, or which reinforcers need to be changed.

7. Giving each reinforcement program several weeks trial before determining success or failure. Expect behavior to change or possibly get worse before seeing improvement.

These programs typically focus on adults in the child's environment and consult with the children only to identify appropriate reinforcers.[3,4]

Effectiveness of Behavior Management Programs

Most studies of behavioral management programs focus on parents trained in behavior management methods for programs conducted with their children. These programs generally have been effective, with the children demonstrating significant improvements in home and school behavior. [3,7,8,82]

Cognitive-Behavioral Theories

self-talk— *talking yourself through new situations or difficult situations by giving verbal instructions to yourself*

self-reinforcement— *providing or deciding upon one's own reinforcement or reward following the completion of a task*

Cognitive-behavioral strategies use reinforcement principles to alter thoughts or cognitions related to ADHD behaviors. Cognitive-behavioral treatment goals involve increasing children's ability to solve problems and monitor their own behaviors. Strategies include teaching the child *self-talk*, goal-setting, problem-solving, and *self-reinforcement* These interventions help children generalize learning behaviors to any number of situations and develop self-control over impulsive behaviors. Methods for teaching these strategies include having the therapist model a behavior, role-play, or having children practice directly using a specific task. Types of tasks vary and may involve solving arithmetic problems, putting together a puzzle, building a model, or role-playing social situations.

The following is an example of a cognitive-behavioral therapy approach:

Tasks are first modeled, then directed by the therapist. As practice trials continue, the child takes increasing control as they learn to instruct and reinforce themselves.

> A child watches a therapist complete a math problem. As the therapist works, he or she uses positive self-talk saying, "...keep trying, remember it takes time to get it right." The therapist may also verbalize step-by-step directions to complete the problem such as, "...now I need to carry the number here, then put in the decimal point...." The child then attempts a problem, with directions and positive feedback from the therapist. Over time, the child begins to make these types of statements with decreasing prompts from the therapist. Eventually, the child uses these techniques spontaneously while doing classwork.

Cognitive-Behavioral Treatment Methods

Because of the differences in cognitive-behavioral treatment for children and adults, this section will be divided in two parts:

* Child treatment (reflects most of the research and development focus to date)

- Adult treatment (reflects a different application of the methods used with children)

Child Treatment Strategies—This section will address the treatment approach and efficacy for:

- Parent Training
- Classroom Therapy
- Self-Contained Therapy
- Academic Skills Therapy
- Social Skills Therapy

A brief discussion of the efficacy of cognitive-behavioral treatments in general follows the discussions of treatment approaches and appears on page 66.

Parent Training—This approach has been a popular treatment for ADHD primarily because the way parents interact and respond to a child with ADHD can significantly impact the course of the child's disorder. Additionally, parents can often provide reinforcement or motivation to get a child to focus on a task for which they have little interest.

The most common use of Parent Training is to combine it with a comprehensive behavior management program.[3]

Parent training involves:

1. **Learning about ADHD**—This part of the training involves discussing ADHD symptoms, possible causes, and treatment. While trainers emphasize the multidimensional causes of ADHD, they focus mostly on the viewpoints that stress biological and inborn *temperament* causes. In this environment, parents are more willing to manage and cope with a chronic disability rather than feeling guilty about their child's behavior.

temperament— an individual's general disposition including emotional reactions, mood shifts, and levels of sensitivity

2. **Focusing on Parent/Child Relations**—This focus addresses both the effect of the child's actions and temperament on the parents as well as the parents' actions and temperament on the child. For example, when parents attempts to change a child's disruptive behavior are unsuccessful, the parents may feel that, "Nothing helps," "He will never change," or "She does it on purpose because she knows how mad I get." These thoughts and feelings can profoundly affect the parent/child relationship. Those in group

parent training often benefit from discussions about these feelings as they find out that they are not alone in their struggles.

During this phase of parent training, cognitive techniques are often utilized. Examples of cognitive techniques used in parent training include:

- Analyzing irrational thoughts (e.g., "He should remember to do his chores without me telling him.")

- Looking for evidence that disputes those thoughts (e.g., "He sometimes remembers to do his chores, and he doesn't forget on purpose.")

- Reframing the situation or thinking about the situation from a different perspective (e.g., "Would I want to clean up dog poop rather than play?")

Additionally, therapists pay attention to how stressful the child's chronic disability can be for the family, how the family copes with these stresses, and how the situation affects various family relationships.

Parents learn how to make simple and clear requests of their children, such as, "In ten minutes, you will need to go to bed," instead of, "You need to go to bed soon."

3. ***Improving Communication Skills***—Parents learn to communicate their feelings and requests to their children without creating conflict. For example, a parent might say, "I don't like it when you yell to get my attention, and so I will ignore you. What I would like you to do is tap me on my arm." Clear communication skills include direct, specific descriptions of the desired behavior and potential consequences for the child rather than merely criticizing the child's problem behavior. This also helps parents clarify what is important.

4. ***Understanding Behavior Management Principles***— This education focuses on how parent responses to behavior either increase or decrease desired behaviors based on the behavioral principles outlined on page 54. Parents receive training in the following areas:

- **Behavioral Reinforcement**—This area focuses on analyzing the child's behaviors and parental responses to those behaviors. In addition, it helps parents consciously reward desired behaviors and discourage unwanted behaviors. These behaviors need to be broken down into components of overall goals (e.g., completion of specific chores and a prescribed bedtime routine indicate an overall ability to comply with rules.)

  Behaviors targeted for modification must be specific, clear, and measurable.

- **Use of Reinforcers**—Therapists identify appropriate reinforcers for each target behavior and generally divide these reinforcers into reinforcement or punishment (or those that increase behavior versus those that discourage a target behavior.) The choices are limitless; positive reinforcers (rewards) can be as basic as food or as complex as earning points for privileges. Punishment may involve the withdrawal of privileges, a requirement to complete extra chores, or a loss of points related to earning money or some other positive reinforcer. Reinforcement requires consistent application to each behavioral incident or time interval. More complex systems may use charts, points, or stars for measuring target behaviors.

  Reinforcers may need to be changed periodically to maintain motivation. In addition, target behaviors need to be reinforced frequently enough so that the child experiences success. Two or three target behaviors can be modified at the same time. Before new goal behaviors are added, the child needs to have consistent success.

  Reinforcers must be important to the child. Some children may not care whether they can stay up late; thus, the privilege has no power to change behavior.

- **Time Out**—Parents are taught that time out must be applied consistently and is more effective if the length of time and place are preset. One reminder may be given as a cue to the child.

- **Increasing Attending Skills**—Because attending skills are critical in shaping children's behavior, this area of behavior management training involves altering the manner in which parents pay attention to their children. Important

benign— mild, harmless

Using observation, therapists find that many parents who believe that they regularly engage in attending skills actually direct or guide their child in some manner during these sessions.

Positive attention entails learning to look for (or attend to) desirable behaviors rather than being "on the lookout" for problems.

By ignoring a behavior, the child receives no reinforcement. Thus, the parent's behavior increases the chances that the child's behavior will decrease.

attending skills include listening, providing positive attention, and ignoring *benign* behavior.

To listen effectively, parents need to spend time talking with children and paying attention to positive aspects without correction, direction, or suggestion. This allows a child to feel noticed and appreciated without any potentially negative interactions. These skills are generally difficult, and parents may begin with short periods of time until they become more comfortable.

Training in positive attention techniques helps parents look for and focus on positive behaviors they want their child to increase or continue. Desirable behaviors need to be noticed more frequently than the child's disruptive behaviors. For example, parents would be asked to pay attention to the times their child readily complies with a request to get ready for bed. This exercise requires the parents to interrupt their own activities to reinforce compliance more often than they attend to (reinforce) non-compliant behavior.

When the parent is asked to ignore unacceptable benign behavior, they are practicing the behavioral principle of extinction. For example, when children whine to get what they want, parents can simply ignore the whining. Parents should then respond positively when a child asks for something in a more acceptable manner. Over time, the whining will subside if reinforcement only occurs for alternative behavior.

Effectiveness of Parent Training—Parent training has demonstrated some effectiveness in reducing parenting stress and increasing parents' self-esteem. Research shows that this increase in parental self-esteem has a positive impact on the child's ADHD symptoms.[83]

Classroom Behavior Management

Although similar to home-based training programs, classroom behavior management often targets different behaviors. For example, teachers may want to reinforce students for remaining in their seats, bringing appropriate materials to class, or raising their hands before talking. In addition, teachers can reinforce the learning of cognitive-behavioral strategies such as self-talk or problem-solving. For example, teachers may remind students to talk their way through math problems, or they may request that children repeat calming phrases to themselves.

Because of the limited time teachers have to spend with individual students, these behavior management programs often suffer from a resulting lack of consistency. This problem can be mitigated by close coordination between home and school. To coordinate behavior management, teachers may develop a daily report card using a point system, checks, or stars for communicating school behavior and goal completion to parents. Often having the child consistently bring the report card to and from school becomes a primary goal. Based on the report card, parents can positively reinforce the child's success at school through verbal praise or other rewards.

Effectiveness of Classroom Behavior Management—Studies have shown these programs to be effective for improving classroom behavior as well as compliance at home.[3,7,8,82] However, the children studied did not attain normal levels of functioning, and this approach was generally less effective than stimulant treatment. In addition, long-term changes and generalization to other situations have yet to be demonstrated. The lack of definitive results may relate to the time and energy needed for parents and teachers to obtain successful behavior management consistency.

Self-Contained Treatment Programs

Self-contained treatment programs are generally used in specialized classrooms or inpatient treatment facilities. These programs involve a more intensive, structured form of behavior management, frequently using a formalized point or token system that assigns a value to behaviors. For example,

These programs overcome the problems of limited consistency and thoroughness prominent with home and classroom management.

students in a special classroom may earn a point each time they raise their hand or follow an instruction (e.g., beginning to write or opening a book). Students may lose a point when they speak out without raising their hand or use profanity. Students may be able to "buy" free time or small objects with their points at the end of the day.

Inpatient treatment facilities utilize this type of treatment program with groups to facilitate communication or social skills. Token systems in these settings may also include different levels of reinforcement frequency. For example, a child may earn or lose points hourly for program or task compliance. These points in turn may combine to determine a daily reward. The ability to earn daily rewards may determine a weekly "level" for general privileges such as a later bed-time, reduced supervision, or even home visits. Inpatient settings offer the consistency missing from classroom or home-based programs because the behavior management system operates 24 hours a day.

Effectiveness of Self-Contained Treatment Programs—

Research indicates that self-contained treatment programs can be as effective as stimulant medication; however, the lack of control of the child's behavior outside the special setting continues to limit effectiveness. Researchers have had greater success with negative consequences (such as point loss) than positive attention and praise. In addition, these studies found that with gradual withdrawal of negative consequences (instead of positive reinforcers) the behavior could be main-tained.[3,8]

Academic Skill Therapies

Children with ADHD demonstrate impaired school perfor-mance on a number of levels. As a result, programs designed to teach academic skills need to target both specific and general skills training and/or remediation. Specific skills taught might include reading, math, or spelling. General skills training should include:

- Organization skills
- Study skills
- Note-taking
- Self-monitoring of behavior and errors

These skills are generally taught in special classes or by individual tutors using cognitive-behavioral strategies. *Peer tutoring* can increase the frequency and immediacy of feedback for children with ADHD.

Effectiveness of Academic Skill Therapies—To date, little research has been conducted in this area, but preliminary results of recent studies based on individual case studies are promising.[84]

peer tutoring— having another student work one-on-one with the student with ADHD

Social Skills Training

Social Skills training relies on theories that social interactions play an important role in ADHD. For instance, when children do not know how to wait their turns or compromise while playing with others, they are likely to be rejected. This rejection can lead to anger or depression. These feelings may be acted on inappropriately by fighting or withdrawal, making the problem worse. When children repeatedly fail in social settings, they may also develop negative associations with schoolwork or getting along with peers.

Social skills training has been incorporated into many school programs as well as both inpatient and outpatient therapy settings.

Social skills interventions generally utilize cognitive-behavioral techniques that focus on social situations. Because aggression appears to be the strongest factor leading to peer rejection, therapy focuses on controlling aggressive behaviors by altering hostile interpretations of events and increasing appropriate coping skills. For instance:

> A boy waiting in line suddenly gets pushed from behind. An impulsive response might be for the child to turn around and hit the person behind him.

Social skills training might involve identifying possible reasons for this event (e.g., the other person tripped or was not paying attention). In this program, the facilitator would present and discuss with students alternatives like talking to the person, talking to a teacher, or ignoring the shove.

Typically conducted in a group setting, Social Skills training generally involves:

- Interaction skills
- Problem-Solving

Typical problems used in Social Skills training can be social situations (e.g., getting along with peers during team sports or waiting turns) or specific tasks (e.g., completing homework or getting to school on time).

- Conflict Resolution
- Anger Management

Interaction Skills—Interaction skills include those necessary for any social interaction with peers, parents, or other adults. Saying "hello," making an introduction to someone new, controlling voice tone, "asking" rather than "telling," making conversation with parents during dinner, making a request of a teacher, and asking peers to join a game are some examples of skills that often need to be addressed. Methods used to teach these skills include practice (either through role-play, having a conversation about a specific topic, or completing a group project), modeling (watching others), and discussion (to increase understanding of behaviors and to generalize to other situations).

Problem-Solving—These skills can be taught to children or adolescents using various methods. Training focuses first on developing solutions to problems typical for the age group presented and then modelling and rehearsing those solutions. Specific activities include:

- Listing probable outcomes (consequences) for the varying solutions
- Determining pros and cons for each solution
- Listing how each solution affects other people
- Rehearsing and refining group-determined solutions for implementation

Conflict Resolution—This component involves teaching children basic and appropriate communication skills that allow them to state their viewpoints and clearly make requests. This approach helps those with ADHD focus on the present and future as well as what they want rather than what they dislike. By having children describe past situations in which conflict existed, alternative solutions can be developed and rehearsed.

In addition to teaching communication skills, this approach helps teach children how to share, wait, take turns, and control impulsiveness. For example, the therapist can have a child practice specific impulse control strategies, such as counting to 10, taking three breaths, or cognitive rehearsal (e.g., saying to themselves "I can wait," or "It will be my turn soon.").

Anger Management—This approach involves helping children or adolescents identify situations that make them angry. Once clients identify these situations, they can discuss thoughts that increase the anger (called "hot thoughts") as well as alternative thoughts less likely to produce anger (called "cool thoughts").

For example, an adolescent may say, "I get angry when I can't go out with my friends." "Hot thoughts" associated with this situation might be, "I never get to do anything," or "They just want to see me miserable; they really don't care about me." To use anger management, the therapist asks the client to rate such thoughts on a scale of 1 to 10 for how angry the person feels when thinking them. "Cool thoughts" are then generated, such as, "I don't get to do what I want sometimes, and I don't like it," or "I know my parents care about me, but I don't like their decisions." These thoughts are then rated on a scale of 1 to 10 as to how angry they make the client feel.

After identifying anger-provoking situations as well as "hot" and "cool" thoughts related to those situations, specific anger management strategies are reviewed. These strategies include:

- Leaving the situation before blowing up
- Taking deep breaths
- Counting to ten
- Asking a friend or teacher for help
- Keeping a journal
- Writing an angry letter that doesn't get mailed
- Playing a sport
- Engaging in regular physical activity to release built up energy

Effectiveness of Social Skills Training—The results of social skills training interventions have been mixed. Some studies have noted short-term changes. Other studies have found positive results evident to teachers or parents, but not to peers.[7] One study used an inpatient setting to train social-cognitive skills using role-playing within groups as well as performance-based feedback and reinforcement throughout the day. The study reported positive results with clients having increased social skills and reduced loneliness at a one-year follow-up.[85]

Others have suggested that including Social Skills Training in Parent Training greatly increases effectiveness.[64] This approach would increase parents' awareness and understanding of the reasons and content of social training for the child, teaching parents techniques that enhance children's learning on a daily basis, and encouraging parents to help their children structure their social lives.

Effectiveness of Cognitive-Behavioral Approaches (in General)

Cognitive-behavioral strategies appear more effective with older children who have reached a higher level of cognitive development.

Cognitive-behavioral strategies used alone have demonstrated limited usefulness and no long-term benefits. The strategies that appear most effective include repeated rehearsal and general problem-solving skills rather than self-instruction and self-monitoring.[8,7] These procedures are effective with older children who have received another type of initial therapy (such as stimulant medication) that controls behavior and attention enough to facilitate using cognitive-behavioral strategies.

Cognitive-Behavioral Treatment for Adults

Adult therapy differs greatly from therapy with children. Generally, children do not choose to participate in treatment, and much of the focus centers on parent training. Although adults usually seek treatment on their own, they may do so because of another presenting problem (e.g., chronic difficulties with employment or relationships, or poor emotional adjustment.)[16] Therapy may be more productive as adults may have a greater capacity for reflection and insight. Therapy for adults with ADHD uses similar methods as therapy with children; however, these techniques are applied differently. These techniques help adults with ADHD:

- Learning about ADHD
- Examining existing coping strategies
- Improving relationships
- Using behavior management principles
- Employing cognitive strategies
- Learning relaxation techniques

Learning about ADHD—Just as children and parents have questions and misconceptions about the disorder, adults with

ADHD want to learn about possible causes, symptoms, and treatment. This knowledge helps them feel some control over their lives, rather than feeling helpless and frustrated.[16]

Examining existing coping strategies—It is important to acknowledge and understand what methods clients have developed for themselves, to evaluate how well these methods work, and decide what needs improvement or change. This process can help give clients a sense of accomplishment and encouragement important for them to continue making changes.

Improving relationships—This part of therapy focuses on significant relationships in the client's life. Therapists teach communication skills (such as discussing feelings, making requests, and being clear and specific) and discuss the impact of ADHD symptoms on others. In these discussions, themes often emerge regarding difficulty with others because of disorganization. For example, someone who is always late for a date and forgets their checkbook may blame others for being too rigid and angry, or feels hopeless about ever having an intimate relationship. Understanding the other person's point of view, and learning to discuss scheduling or ask for reminders can improve relationships.

Using behavior management principles—Many principles of behavior management apply to self-reinforcement (it's hard to ignore yourself). Several principles can help self-reinforce certain behaviors. For example, clients can reward themselves for completing a project with a special dinner or a fun activity. Or, they might allow themselves to watch the news or a television show only after completing housework. They also might set up a "punishment" by charging themselves or donating a specified amount of money every time they are late to work or an appointment.

Employing cognitive strategies—Cognitive strategies can help clients with organizational skills and self-talk. Organizational skills may include:

- Using a calender to show assignments or meetings

- Breaking a task into small steps of 15-30 minute periods

Clients can use cognitive strategies to adjust their work environment by:

- *Getting an answering machine and turning off the volume*

- *Playing a tape with white noise*

- *Wearing headphones*

- *Pinning up pictures or quotations for inspiration*

- *Making a study carrel*

- *Using a Do Not Disturb sign*

- *Buying special pens, paper, or other supplies*

- Set starting, midpoint, and finishing dates for long projects (and set the finish date ahead of the actual deadline)

- Adjusting the work environment to minimize distractions and enhance enjoyment[16]

As with children, self-talk can increase adult feelings of control and a belief that they can accomplish what they want. Self-talk may consist either of positive self-statements ("Keep trying; you can do it,") or self-directions (e.g., "For learning to tie a new knot, first, make two loops with the string, then make a circle, now pull the top one through.").

Learning relaxation techniques—A number of techniques exist for helping people relax, which may increase concentration and lessen impulsivity. For example, progressive muscle relaxation involves tensing and relaxing different muscle groups. *Meditation* or *yoga* can help increase relaxation and focus. *Imagery* may help a client visualize themselves after accomplishing a task and increase motivation, or to see a favorite quiet spot where they can reenergize themselves. Although utilized by many people, there is no current research on efficacy for these techniques.

meditation— an activity that combines relaxation with focusing one's thoughts

yoga— a system of exercises for attaining bodily or mental control

imagery— the use of mental images

An Integrated Approach to ADHD Therapy

The most effective approach to environmentally based therapy seems to involve integration of developmental and behavioral theories. The following examples clarify how a theorist uses an integrated approach to view ADHD from several perspectives (indicated in parentheses).

- An extremely active infant requiring high levels of attention may fare better if "matched" (family systems) with stimulating, active parents who reinforce positive behavior (behavioral) and minimize negative behavior.

- If a high-activity infant is matched with a disorganized home environment or low-energy parents (family systems), the parents may respond to disruptive behaviors impulsively and reinforce them, modelling impulsivity to the child (behavioral).

- As parents' patience with and energy for the child become taxed, the bond between parents and child weakens, and negative responses between them occur more frequently (attachment theory).

- Increasing use of day care can bring additional stress on a family. As the child's time with parents decreases and day care provider complaints about the child's disruptive behavior and potential aggression increase, positive relationships are further disrupted which may sustain ADHD behavior (attachment theory).

Recent research has demonstrated some evidence for using an integrated theoretical approach, especially among low socioeconomic status families at high risk for emotional or physical problems.[3,8] Negative, harsh parenting and intrusiveness tend to increase current and future impulsivity and hyperactivity. Because researching these types of psychosocial factors is problematic due to the inability to cleanly separate study variables, further research needs to be conducted before drawing any conclusions.[3,8] For example, a negative parenting style may be a reaction to a difficult child, a result of poor parenting skills, or an inherited impulsivity of the parents. This integrated theoretical approach has led to a greater focus on multimodal treatment techniques that combine treatment strategies.

Multimodal interventions need to occur early, with long-term treatment and follow-up to address changing needs or problems in relationships, academics, or at home, as the individual matures.

Multimodal Treatment

Multimodal interventions most commonly include behavior and drug therapies and focus on:

- Behavioral reinforcement
- Cognitive-behavioral techniques for problem-solving
- Medication therapy
- Family therapy

Effectiveness of Multimodal Approaches

Several studies report a slight increase in efficacy when treatments combine medication and psychotherapy; however, the advantage of this approach over the use of medication alone appears slight.[3,8,86] Methodological shortcomings in these studies included problems with how the behavior

69

therapy was conducted and the lack of reported long-term outcomes. At this point, there are several large-scale investigations underway to correct these flaws. Until these investigations are completed, therapists generally agree that utilizing a multimodal treatment, when possible, affords children and adults the best opportunity to learn control and alter the course of ADHD.[3,8]

Therapy Notes from the Desk of Pat Owen

Completed three months of psychotherapy with T.J. and family. T.J. has shown improvement in school with grades now in the average and low-average range. Academic Skills therapy with an individual tutor helped. Decreased fighting at school, perhaps resulting from the cognitive-behavioral social skills therapy. Worked with mother on behavior reinforcement program at home which has increased T.J.'s compliance and time spent on homework. Mother is also better at communicating clearly, with more reasonable expectations and a sense of being able to keep the family organized and under control. Recommend continued use of stimulant medication as well as T.J.'s continued involvement in extracurricular activities in order to increase his sense of accomplishment and self-esteem.

Appendix A: ADHD Interview

Name of Child _____   Interview Date _____

Interviewer _____   Informant _____

Reason for Referral:

(The reason for referral may discriminate an acute vs. chronic problem, reveal motivation for treatment, highlight family stressors or other family circumstances that may help in diagnosis.)

Referral Source:

Parental Objectives (goals for treatment or assessment):

(1) I. Developmental Factors (PRIVATE)

   A. Prenatal History

   1. How was your health during pregnancy?

Good	____	(1)
Fair	____	(3)
Poor	____	(5)
DK	____	

   2. How old were you when your child was born?

Under 20	____	(1)
20-24	____	(2)
25-29	____	(3)
30-34	____	(4)
35-39	____	(5)
40-44	____	(6)
Over 44	____	(7)
DK	____	

Do you recall using any of the following substances or medications during pregnancy?

   3. Beer or Wine **(2)**

Never	____	(1)
Once or twice	____	(2)
3-9 times	____	(3)
10-19 times	____	(4)
20-39 times	____	(5)
40+ times	____	(6)

   4. Hard liquor

Never	____	(1)
Once or twice	____	(2)
3-9 times	____	(3)
10-19 times	____	(4)
20-39 times	____	(5)
40+ times	____	(6)

   5. Coffee or other caffeine (Cokes, etc.) **(3)** Taken together, how may times?

Never	____	(1)
Once or twice	____	(2)
3-9 times	____	(3)
10-19 times	____	(4)
20-39 times	____	(5)
40+ times	____	(6)

NOTES:

(1) It is important to remember that any signs of risk or predisposing factors, by themselves or in combination, do not mean the client is doomed; they are only "warning bells" or confirming evidence.

(2) Abuse of alcohol can be a predisposing factor in ADHD, Fetal Alcohol Syndrome, or other developmental disorders.

(3) Use of drugs, including caffeine, can have an impact on a fetus; specific effects are unclear.

(4) 6.   Cigarettes
Never _____ (1)
Once or twice _____ (2)
3-9 times _____ (3)
10-19 times _____ (4)
20-39 times _____ (5)
40+ times _____ (6)

7.   Did you ingest any of the following
substances?
Valium (Librium, Xanax) _____
Tranquilizers _____
Antiseizure medications
(e.g., Dilantin) _____
Treatment for diabetes _____
Antibiotics (for viral
infections) _____
Sleeping pills _____
Other (please specify) _____

(5) B. Perinatal History

8.   Did you have toxemia or eclampsia?

9.   Was there Rh factor incompatibility?

10. Was (s)he born on schedule?
8 months or earlier _____ (1)
Term 8-10 mos. _____ (2)
10 mos. _____ (3)
DK _____

11. What was the duration of labor?
Under 6 hr. _____ (1)
7-12 hr. _____ (2)
13-18 hr. _____ (3)
19-24 hr. _____ (4)
Over 24 hr. _____ (5)
DK _____

12. Were you given any drugs to ease the
pain during labor?
Name: _____

No _____ (0)
Yes _____ (1)
DK _____

13. Were there indications of fetal distress
during labor or during birth?
No _____ (0)
Yes _____ (1)
DK _____

14. Was delivery normal?
No _____ (0)
Yes _____ (1)

Breech?
No _____ (0)
Yes _____ (1)

Caesarian?
No _____ (0)
Yes _____ (1)

Forceps? **(6)**
No _____ (0)
Yes _____ (1)

Induced?
No _____ (0)
Yes _____ (1)

15. What was the child's birth weight?
2 lb-3 lb 15 oz _____ (1)
4 lb-5 lb 15 oz _____ (2)
6 lb-7 lb 15 oz _____ (3)
8 lb-9 lb 15 oz _____ (4)
10 lb-11 lb 15 oz _____ (5)
DK _____

16. Were there any health complications
following birth?
No _____ (0)
Yes _____ (1)
If yes, specify: _____

NOTES:

(4) Heavy smoking is associated with the development of ADHD.

(5) Difficulty during birth is a risk factor for ADHD.

(6) Forceps put pressure on soft brain tissue. Although not known specifically to cause ADHD, the possibility of frontal lobe damage contributes to the risk factor.

C. Postnatal Period and Infancy

17. Were there early infancy feeding problems?

No	___	(0)
Yes	___	(1)

18. Was the child colicky?

No	___	(0)
Yes	___	(1)

(7) 19. Were there early infancy sleep pattern difficulties?

No	___	(0)
Yes	___	(1)

(8) 20. Were there problems with the infant's responsiveness (alertness)?

No	___	(0)
Yes	___	(1)

21. Did the child experience any health problems during infancy?

No	___	(0)
Yes	___	(1)

22. Did the child have any congenital problems?

No	___	(0)
Yes	___	(1)

23. Was the child an easy baby? By that, I mean did (s)he follow a schedule fairly well?

Very easy	___	(1)
Easy	___	(2)
Average	___	(3)
Difficult	___	(4)
Very diff.	___	(5)

24. How did the baby behave with other people?

More sociable than average	___	(1)
Average sociability	___	(2)
More unsociable than average	___	(3)

25. When (s)he wanted something, how insistent was (s)he?

Very insistent	___	(1)
Pretty insistent	___	(2)
Average	___	(3)
Not very insistent	___	(4)
Not at all insistent	___	(5)

(9) 26. How would you rate the activity level of the child as an infant/toddler?

Very active	___	(1)
Active	___	(2)
Average	___	(3)
Less active	___	(4)
Not active		(5)

D. Developmental Milestones (10)

27. At what age did (s)he sit up?

3-6 mos.	___	(1)
7-12 mos.	___	(2)
Over 12 mos.	___	(3)
DK	___	

28. At what age did (s)he crawl?

6-12 mos.	___	(1)
13-18 mos.	___	(2)
Over 18 mos.	___	(3)
DK	___	

29. At what age did (s)he walk?

Under 1 yr	___	(1)
1-2 yr	___	(2)
2-3 yr	___	(3)
DK	___	

NOTES:

(7) Disrupted sleeping and eating patterns could signify later ADHD.

(8) Extremes in either direction could reflect ADHD or other developmental difficulties.

(9) A recognizable indicator of later hyperactivity.

(10) Erratic or uneven achievement of developmental milestones is a marker for ADHD.

30. At what age did (s)he speak single words (other than "mama" or "dada")?

9-13 mos.	___	(1)
14-18 mos.	___	(2)
19-24 mos.	___	(3)
25-36 mos.	___	(4)
37-48 mos.	___	(5)
DK	___	

31. At what age did (s)he string two or more words together?

9-13 mos.	___	(1)
14-18 mos.	___	(2)
19-24 mos.	___	(3)
25-36 mos.	___	(4)
37-48 mos.	___	(5)
DK	___	

32. At what age was (s)he toilet-trained? (Bladder Control)

Under 1 yr	___	(1)
1-2 yr	___	(2)
3-4 yr	___	(3)
DK	___	

33. At what age was (s)he toilet-trained? (Bowel Control)

Under 1 yr	___	(1)
1-2 yr	___	(2)
3-4 yr	___	(3)
DK	___	

34. Approximately how much time did toilet training take from onset to completion?

Less than 1 mo.	___	(1)
1-2 mos.	___	(2)
2-3 mos.	___	(3)
More than 3 mos.	___	(4)

II. Medical History

35. How would you describe his/her health? ⑪

Very good	___	(1)
Good	___	(2)
Fair	___	(3)
Poor	___	(4)
Very Poor	___	(5)

36. How is his/her hearing?

Good	___	(1)
Fair	___	(2)
Poor	___	(3)

37. How is her/her vision?

Good	___	(1)
Fair	___	(2)
Poor	___	(3)

38. How is his/her gross motor coordination? ⑫

Good	___	(1)
Fair	___	(2)
Poor	___	(3)

39. How is his/her fine motor coordination?

Good	___	(1)
Fair	___	(2)
Poor	___	(3)

40. How is his/her speech articulation?

Good	___	(1)
Fair	___	(2)
Poor	___	(3)

41. Has (s)he had any chronic health problems (e.g., asthma, diabetes, heart condition?

No	___	(0)
Yes	___	(1)

NOTES:

⑪ Certain health problems or illnesses may impact behavior, or reflect a medical basis for behavior problems.

⑫ Children with ADHD often appear clumsy because of their impulsivity. True delays in motor skills may need formal assessment.

If yes, please
   specify?_____

42. When was the onset of any chronic
    illness?

Birth	___	(1)
0-1 yr	___	(2)
1-2 yr	___	(5)
2-3 yr	___	(3)
3-4 yr	___	(4)
Over 4 yr	___	

43. Which of the following illnesses has
    the child had?
(For the following, No= 0; Yes= 1)

Mumps	___
Chicken pox	___
Measles	___
Whooping cough	___
Scarlet fever	___
Pneumonia	___
Encephalitis	___
Otitis media	___
(13) Lead poisoning	___
Seizures	___
Other diseases	___
(specify)_____	

(14) 44. Has the child had any accidents
    resulting in the following?
(No= 0; Yes= 1)

Broken bones	___
Severe lacerations	___
Head injury	___
Severe bruises	___
Stomach Pumped	___
Eye injury	___
Lost teeth	___
Sutures	___
Other (specify)	___

45. How many accidents?

One	___	(1)
2-3	___	(2)
4-7	___	(3)
8-12	___	(4)
Over 12	___	(5)

46. Has (s)he ever had surgery for any of
    the following conditions?
    (No= 0; Yes= 1)

Tonsillitis	___
Adenoids	___
Hernia	___
Appendicitis	___
Eye, ear, nose, & throat	___
Digestive disorder	___
Urinary tract	___
Leg or arm	___
Burns	___
Other	___

47. How many times?

Once	___	(1)
Twice	___	(2)
3-5 times	___	(3)
6-8 times	___	(4)
Over 8 times	___	(5)

48. Duration of hospitalization?

One day	___	(1)
One day + night	___	(2)
2-3 days	___	(3)
4-6 days	___	(4)
1-4 weeks	___	(5)
1-2 mos.	___	(6)
Over 2 mos.	___	(7)

49. Is there any suspicion of alcohol or (15)
    drug use?

No	___	(0)
Yes	___	(1)
DK	___	

NOTES:

(13) Lead poisoning can result in signs of ADHD.

(14) Children with ADHD are frequently accident-prone.

(15) Erratic behavior could be in response to factors such as substance use, or physical or sexual abuse.

75

50. Is there any history of physical/
    sexual abuse?

No   ___   (0)
Yes   ___   (1)
DK   ___

(16) 51. Does the child have any problems
    sleeping?

None   ___   (0)
Difficulty falling
  asleep   ___   (1)
Sleep continuity
  disturbance   ___   (2)
Early morning
  awakening   ___   (3)

52. Is the child a restless sleeper?
No   ___   (0)
Yes   ___   (1)

(17) 53. Does the child have bladder control
    problems at night?
No   ___   (0)
Yes   ___   (1)
  If yes, how often? ___
  If yes, was (s)he ever continent?___

During the day?
No   ___   (0)
Yes   ___   (1)
  If yes, how often? ___
  If yes, was (s)he ever continent?___

54. Does the child have bowel control
    problems at night?

No   ___   (0)
Yes   ___   (1)
  If yes, how often? ___
  If yes, was (s)he ever continent?___

During the day?
No   ___   (0)
Yes   ___   (1)
  If yes, how often? ___
  If yes, was (s)he ever continent?___

(18) 55. Does the child have any appetite
    control problems?
Overeats   ___   (1)
Average   ___   (2)
Undereats   ___   (3)

III. Treatment History

56. Has the child ever been prescribed
    any of the following?
(No= 0; Yes= 1)
(Duration coded in months)
Ritalin   ___   **(19)**
  Duration of Use   ___
Dexedrine   ___
  Duration of Use   ___
Cylert   ___
  Duration of Use   ___
Tranquilizers   ___
  Duration of Use   ___
Anticonvulsants   ___
  Duration of Use   ___
Antihistamines   ___
  Duration of Use   ___
Other prescription drugs   ___
  Duration of Use   ___
  Specify: _____

(20) 57. Has the child ever had any of the
    following forms of psychological
    treatment? If so, how long did it last?
Individual psychotherapy   ___
  Duration of therapy   ___
Group Psychotherapy   ___
  Duration of therapy   ___

NOTES:

(16) Sleep disturbance can indicate ADHD, Depression, or other psychological concerns.

(17) Bed-wetting is a risk factor for ADHD, but could indicate other disturbances.

(18) This could be a sign of psychological distress, poor coping, or an eating disorder.

(19) Past use of Ritalin does not automatically indicate ADHD; previous diagnoses could be inaccurate.

(20) Get information about the reason for treatment, goals, and progress

76

Family therapy with child ____
  Duration of therapy ____
Inpatient evaluation/Rx ____
  Duration of inpatient stay ____
Residential treatment ____
  Duration of placement ____

IV. School History

(21) Please summarize the child's progress (e.g., academic, social, testing) within each of these grade levels:

Preschool
Grades 4 thru 6
Kindergarten
Grades 7 thru 12
Grades 1 thru 3

58. Has the child ever been in any type of special educational program, and if so, how long?
Learning disabilities class ____
  Duration of placement ____
Behavioral/emotional
  disorders class ____
  Duration of placement ____
Resource room ____
  Duration of placement ____
Speech & language therapy ____
  Duration of therapy ____
Other (Specify) _____
  Duration ____

59. Has the child ever been:
Suspended from school ____
  Number of suspensions ____
Expelled from school ____
  Number of expulsions ____
Retained in grade ____
  Number of retentions ____

60. Have any additional instructional modifications been attempted?
None ____ (0)
Behavior modification
  program ____ (1)
Daily/weekly report
  card ____ (2)
Other (please specify) ____ (3) (22)

V. Social History

61. How does the child get along with his/her brothers/sisters?
Doesn't have any ____ (0)
Better than
  average ____ (1)
Average ____ (2)
Worse than average ____ (3)

62. How easily does the child make friends?
Easier than average ____ (1)
Average ____ (2)
Worse than average ____ (3)
DK ____ (4)

63. On the average, how long does your child keep friendships?
Less than 6 months ____ (1)
6 months-1 year ____ (2)
More than 1 year ____ (3)
DK ____

VI. Current Behavioral Concerns

Primary concerns _____

_____

Other (related) concerns _____

_____

NOTES:

(21) This information is important not only to establish a pattern over time, but also for differential diagnosis of ODD or learning disabilities.

(22) Impaired peer relationships is a marker for ADHD.

77

(23) 64. What strategies have been imple-
mented to address these problems?
(Check which have been successful)

Verbal reprimands ___ (1)
Time out (isolations) ___ (2)
Removal of privileges ___ (3)
Rewards ___ (4)
Physical punishment ___ (5)
Acquiescence to child ___ (6)
Avoidance to child ___ (7)

65. On the average, what percentage of
the time does your child initially
comply with commands?

0-20 percent ___ (1)
20-40 percent ___ (2)
40-60 percent ___ (3)
60-80 percent ___ (4)
80-100 percent ___ (5)

66. On the average, what percentage of
the time does your child eventually
comply with commands?

0-20 percent ___ (1)
20-40 percent ___ (2)
40-60 percent ___ (3)
60-80 percent ___ (4)
80-100 percent ___ (5)

67. To what extent are you and your
spouse consistent with respect to
disciplinary strategies?

Most of the time ___ (1)
Some of the time ___ (2)
None of the time ___ (3)

(24) 68. Have any of the following stress
events occurred within the past 12
months?

Parents divorced or
separated ___ (1)
Family accident or
illness ___ (2)

Death in family ___ (3)
Parent changed job ___ (4)
Changed schools ___ (5)
Family moved ___ (6)
Family financial
problems ___ (7)
Other (please specify) ___ (8)

VIII. Diagnostic Criteria

69. Which of the following are considered to be a significant problem at the
present time?
(No= 0; Yes= 1)

(Inattention)
Fails to give close attention
to details or makes careless
mistakes ___
Has difficulty sustaining
attention in tasks or play
activities ___
Does not seem to listen
when spoken to directly ___
Does not follow through
on instructions and fails
to finish tasks ___
Has difficulty organizing
tasks and activities ___
Avoids tasks that require
sustained mental effort
such as schoolwork or
homework ___
Loses things necessary for
tasks or activities ___
Is easily distracted by
extraneous stimuli ___
Is forgetful in daily activities ___

TOTAL for **inattention**
=(6 or more) ___

NOTES:

(23) This can reveal information regarding current parenting styles, pertinent family dynamics, or differential
diagnosis (ODD vs. ADHD).

(24) These stressors could contribute to behavior changes

(Hyperactivity-Impulsivity)

Fidgets with hands or feet or
squirms in seat ___
Leaves seat when remaining
seated is expected ___
Runs about, moves, or climbs
excessively in situations when
it is inappropriate ___
Has difficulty engaging in
leisure activities quietly ___
Is often "on the go" or acts as
if "driven by a motor" ___
Often talks excessively ___

Often blurts out answers
before questions have
been completed ___
Often has difficulty
awaiting turn ___
Often interrupts or intrudes
on others ___

TOTAL for **hyperactivity-
impulsivity**=(6 or more) ___

70. When did these problems begin?
(Specify age): _____

71. Which of the following are consid-
ered to be a significant problem at the
present time.
(No= 0; Yes= 1)
Often loses temper ___
Often argues with adults ___
Often actively defies or refuses
adult requests of rules ___
Often deliberately
annoys people ___
Often blames others for his/
her mistakes or misbehavior ___
Is often touchy or easily
annoyed by others ___
Is often angry or resentful ___
Is often spiteful or vindictive ___

TOTAL for **Oppositional Defiant
Disorder** = (4 or more) ___

72. When did these problems begin?
(Specify age): ___

73. Which of the following are considered
to be a significant problem at the
present time?
(No= 0; Yes= 1)
Bullies, threatens, or
intimidates others ___
Initiates physical fights ___
Used a weapon ___
Physically cruel ___
Has been physically cruel
to animals ___
Stolen with confrontation ___
Forced someone into
sexual activity ___
Fire setting with the intent
to damage ___
Deliberately destroyed others'
property (other than
fire-setting) ___
Broken into someone else's
house, building, or car. ___
Lies often ___
Stolen without confrontation ___
Stays out at night,
(before age 13) ___
Run away from home overnight
at least twice, (before age 13) ___

TOTAL for **Conduct Disorder** =
(3 or more) ___

74. When did these problems begin?
(Specify age): ___

75. Which of the following are considered
to be a significant problem at the
present time?
(No= 0; Yes= 1)

Recurrent excessive distress
about separation from home or
major attachment figures ___
Persistent and excessive worry
about possible harm to major
attachment figures ___
Persistent worry that an
untoward event will separate
child from a major attachment
figure ___
Persistent school refusal ___

79

Persistent fear of being
alone at home or without
significant adults in other
settings ____
Persistent refusal to sleep alone ____
Repeated nightmares about
separation ____
Repeated somatic complaints
related to separation ____

TOTAL for **Separation Anxiety
Disorder** =(3 or more) ____

76. When did these problems begin?
(Specify age): ____

77. Which of the following are considered to be a significant problem at
the present time?
(No= 0; Yes= 1)

Restlessness or feeling on edge ____
Fatigued easily ____
Difficulty concentrating ____
Irritability ____
Muscle tension ____
Sleep disturbance ____

TOTAL for **Generalized Anxiety
Disorder** =(1 or more children; 3 or
more adults) ____

78. When did these problems begin?
Specify age): ____

79. Which of the following are considered to be a significant problem at
the present time?
(No= 0; Yes= 1)
(25) Depressed or irritable mood most
of the day, nearly every day ____
(25) Diminished pleasure in
activities ____
Weight loss or gain ____

Insomnia or hypersomnia
nearly every day ____
Psychomotor agitation or
retardation ____
Fatigue or loss of energy ____
Feelings of worthlessness or
inappropriate guilt ____
Diminished ability to
concentrate or indecisiveness ____
Suicidal ideation or attempt ____

TOTAL for **Major Depressive Episode**
(times 3-9) = (5 or more) ____

80. When did these problems begin?
(Specify age): ____

81. Which of the following are considered to be a significant problem at
the present time?
(No= 0; Yes= 1)

(26)

Depressed or irritable mood
for most of the day x 1 yr ____
Poor appetite or overeating ____
Insomnia or hypersomnia ____
Low energy or fatigue ____
Low self-esteem ____
Feelings of hopelessness ____
Never without symptoms for
2 mos. over 1-yr period ____

TOTAL for **Dysthymia** (items 2-7) =
(2 or more) ____

82. When did these problems begin?
(Specify age): ____

VIII.   Other Concerns

83. Has the child exhibited any of the
symptoms below (No= 0; Yes= 1)
Stereotyped mannerisms ____

NOTES:

(25) Need to have one of these plus four of the other criteria to diagnose Major Depression.

(26) Need to have this criteria plus one other to diagnose Dysthymia.

Odd postures ____
Excessive reaction to noise or
  fails to react to loud noise ____
Overreacts to touch ____
Compulsive rituals ____
Motor tics ____
Vocal tics ____
TOTAL = ____

(NOTE: The remaining questions in this section are optional.)

84. Has the child exhibited any symptoms of **thought disturbance**, including any of the following: (No= 0; Yes=1)

Loose thinking (e.g., tangential
  ideas, circumstantial speech) ____
Bizarre ideas (e.g., odd
  fascinations, delusions,
  hallucinations) ____
Disoriented, confused, staring,
  or "spacey" ____
Incoherent speech (mumbles,
  jargon) ____
TOTAL = ____

85. Has the child exhibited any symptoms of **affective disturbance**, including any of the following: (No= 0; Yes= 1)

Excessive lability w/o reference
  to environment ____
Explosive temper with
  minimal provocation ____
Excessive clinging, attachment,
  or dependence on adults ____
Unusual fears ____
Strange aversions ____
Panic attacks ____
Excessively constricted or
  bland affect ____
Situationally inappropriate
  emotions ____
TOTAL = ____

86. Has the child exhibited any symptoms of **social conduct disturbance**, including the following? (No= 0; Yes=1)

Little or no interest in peers ____
Significantly indiscreet
  remarks ____
Initiates or terminates
  interactions inappropriately ____
Qualitatively abnormal
  social behavior ____
Excessive reaction to
  changes in routine ____
Abnormalities of speech ____
Self-mutilation ____
TOTAL = ____

IX. Family History

87. How long have you and the child's father (mother) been married? (Please note whether the child was the product of 1st, 2nd, etc. marriage.)

Never married ____ (0)
Separated ____ (1)
Divorced ____ (2)
Widowed ____ (3)
Married for ___ yrs ____ (4)

88. How stable is your current marriage?

Stable ____ (1)
Unstable ____ (2)

Notes:

Family Members

(Note which family members have experienced the following):

	Self	Mother	Father	Brother	Sister	Total
Problems with aggressiveness, defiance, and oppositional behavior as a child						
Problems with attention, activity, and impulse control as a child						
Learning disabilities						
Failed to graduate from high school						
Mental retardation						
Psychosis or schizophrenia						
Depression for greater than 2 weeks						
Anxiety disorder that impaired adjustment						
Tics or Tourette's						
Alcohol abuse						
Substance abuse						
Antisocial behavior (assaults, thefts, etc.)						
Arrests						
Physical abuse						
Sexual abuse						
0 =Negative; 1= Positive						

82

Glossary

A
autonomy— a sense of independence

B
benign— mild, harmless

biochemical agents— neurotransmitters or chemicals in the brain that affect behavior as well as mood and thought processes

C
cognitive— thinking abilities

CT scan technology— computerized x-ray of the brain

D
delusions— a belief that someone maintains despite much evidence to the contrary. For example, children may persist in believing that they are cartoon characters while adults may believe that they are superhuman.

discriminating power— listed in order of ability to differentiate one disorder from another

disinhibition— the lowering of inhibitions that results in behaviors occurring spontaneously, without thought

dopamine, serotonin, and norepinepherine— chemicals in the brain that help regulate motor-control systems and central nervous system functioning

dysfunction— a disruption in normal functioning

E
euphoria- a sense of extreme elation and heightened activity

executive functions— brain activity involved in the organization and integration of various brain functions

F
Fetal Alcohol Syndrome— abnormal anatomical features and psychological deficits including growth deficiencies, skeletal malformations, mental retardation, hyperactivity, and heart murmurs

G
genetic— chromosomes that influence the development of an organism

H
heritability— the percentage of transmissions of chromosomal links, from one generation to another
I
imagery— the use of mental images

intrauterine— inside the uterus

L

longitudinal research— research on the same people conducted over a period of several years

M

maladaptive behavior— behavior that leads to excessive distress, typically requiring therapy

manifest symptoms— overtly display symptoms

meditation— an activity that combines relaxation with focusing one's thoughts

mirroring and imitation— verbal and nonverbal mimicking of facial expressions, movements, or vocalizations

MRI— Magnetic Resonance Imaging, a radiological process for taking pictures of internal structures

P

peer tutoring— having another student work one-on-one with the student with ADHD

polygenetic— multiple genes involved in the disorder

prognoses— outcome in the future

R

reactivity effects— different behaviors caused by being watched

reinforcement— any consequence that increases the frequency of the preceding behavior

reliable— the extent to which the test produces similar results when administered at different times

S

self-reinforcement— providing or deciding upon one's own reinforcement or reward following the completion of a task

self-talk— talking yourself through new situations or difficult situations by giving verbal instructions to yourself

stigmatizing— a mark on one's reputation

T

temperament— an individual's general disposition including emotional reactions, mood shifts, and levels of sensitivity

V

validity— the extent to which a test measures what it claims to measures

Y

yoga— a system of exercises for attaining bodily or mental control

Bibliography

1. American Psychiatric Association (1994). <u>Diagnostic and statistical manual of mental disorders</u> (4th ed.). Washington, DC: Author

2. Barkley, R.A. (1989). Attention deficit hyperactivity disorder. In E.J. Mash & R.A. Barkley, (Eds.) <u>Treatment of childhood disorders</u> (pp. 39-72). New York: Guilford Press.

3. Barkley, R.A. (1990). <u>Attention-deficit Hyperactivity Disorder: A handbook for diagnosis and treatment</u>. New York: Guilford Press.

4. Fouse, B., & Brians, S. (1993). <u>A primer on attention deficit disorder</u>. Bloomington: Phi Delta Kappa Educational Foundation.

5. Gammon, G.D., Hallowell, E.M., & Ratey, J.J. (1994). <u>Driven to distraction</u>. New York: Pantheon Books.

6. Walters, A.S., & Barrett, R. P. (1993). The history of hyperactivity. In J.L. Matson (Ed.), <u>Handbook of hyperactivity in children</u> (pp. 1-10). Boston: Allyn and Bacon.

7. Weiss, G. & Hechtman, L.T. (1993). <u>Hyperactive children grown up</u> (2nd ed.). New York: Guilford Press.

8. Hinshaw, S.P. (1994). <u>Attention deficits and hyperactivity in children. Thousand Oaks</u>. CA: Sage

9. Lorys-Vernon, A.R., Hynd, G.W., Lyytinen, H., & Hern, K. (1993). Etiology of attention deficit hyperactivity disorder. In J.L. Matson (Ed.), <u>Handbook of hyperactivity in children</u> (pp. 47-65). Boston: Allyn and Bacon.

10. Biederman, J., Faraone, S.V., Spencer, T., Wilens, T., Mick, E., Lapey, K.A. (1994). Gender differences in a sample of adults with attention deficit disorder. <u>Psychiatry Research, 53</u>, 13-29.

11. Campbell, S.B., (1985). Hyperactivity in preschoolers: Correlates and prognostic implications. Special Issue: Attention deficit disorder: Issues in assessment and intervention. <u>Clinical Psychology Review, 5</u>, 405-428

12. Fischer, M., Barkley, R.A., Edelbrock, C.S., & Smallish, L. (1990). The adolescent outcome of hyperactive children diagnosed by research criteria: Academic, attentional, and neuropsychological status. <u>Journal of Consulting and Clinical Psychology, 58</u>, 580-588.

13. McMahon, R.J. (1994). Diagnosis, assessment, and treatment of externalizing problems in children: The role of longitudinal data. <u>Journal of Consulting and Clinical Psychology, 62</u>, 901917

14. Manuzza, S., Klein, R.G., Bessler, A., Malloy, P., Lapadula, M. (1993). Adult outcome of hyperactive boys. <u>Archives of General Psychiatry, 50</u>, 565-576.

15. Manuzza, S., Klein, R.G., Bonagura, N., Malloy, P., Giampino, T.L., & Addalli, K. A. (1991). Hyperactive boys almost grown up: Replication of psychiatric status. Archives of General Psychiatry, 48, 77-83

16. Leimkuhler, M. E. (1994). Attention-deficit disorder in adults and adolescents: Cognitive, behavioral, and personality styles. In J. M. Ellison et al. (Eds.), The psychotherapist's guide to neuropsychiatry: Diagnostic and treatment issues (pp. 175-216). Washington DC: American Psychiatric Press.

17. Editorial (1994). Attention deficit hyperactivity disorder in adults. American Journal of Psychiatry, 151, 633-638.

18. American Psychiatric Association (1987). Diagnostic and statistical manual of mental disorders (3rd ed. rev.). Washington, DC: Author.

19. Erikson, E.H. (1963). Childhood and society (2nd ed.). New York: Norton.

20. Biederman, J., Faraone, S.V., Spencer, T., Wilens, T., Norman, D., Lapey, K.A., Mick, E., Lehman, B.K., Doyle, A. (1993). Patterns of psychiatric comorbidity, cognition, and psychosocial functioning in adults with attention deficit hyperactivity disorder. American Journal of Psychiatry, 150, 1792-1798.

21. Wilens, T. E., & Biederman, J. (1992). The stimulants. Psychiatric Clinics of North America, 15, 191-222.

22. Barkley, R.A. (1988). Attention deficit disorder with hyperactivity. In E.J. Mash & L.G. Terdal, (Eds.) Behavioral assessment of childhood disorders. New York: Guilford Press.

23. Koziol, L.G., Stout, C.E., & Ruben, D.H. (1993). Handbook of childhood impulse disorders and ADHD: Theory and practice. Springfield: C.C. Thomas.

24. Grimley, L.K. (1993). Academic assesment of ADHD children. In J.L. Matson (Ed.), Handbook of hyperactivity in children (pp. 169-185). Boston: Allyn and Bacon.

25. Achenbach, T.M., & Edelbrock, C. (1986). Manual for the Teacher Report Form and the Child Behavior Profile. Burlington: Department of Psychiatry, University of Vermont.

26. DuPaul, G.J. (1990c). Parent and teacher ratings of ADHD symptoms: Psychometric properties in community-based sample. Manuscript submitted for publication, University of Massachusetts Medical Center, Worcester.

27. Klein, D.R., & Gittleman-Klein, R. (1975). Problems in diagnosis of minimal brain dysfunction and the hyperkinetic syndrome. International Journal of Mental Health, 4, 45-60.

28. Platzman, K. A., Stoy, M.R., Brown, R. T., Coles, C. D., et al. (1992). Review of observational methods in attention deficit hyperactivity disorder (ADHD): Implications for diagnosis. School Psychology Quarterly, 7, 155-177.

29. Goyette, C.H., Conners, C.K., & Ulrich, R.F. (1978). Normative data for Revised Conners Parent and Teacher Rating Scales. Journal of Child Psychology, 6, 221-236.

30. Achenbach, T.M., & Edelbrock, C. (1983). <u>Manual for the Child Behavior Checklist and Revised Child Behavior Profile</u>. Burlington: Department of Psychiatry, University of Vermont.

31. Biederman, J., Faraone, S.V., Doyle, A. Lehman, B.K., Kraus, I., Perrin, J., Tsuang, M.T. (1993). Convergence of the Child Behavior Checklist with structured interview-based psychiatric diagnoses of ADHD children with and without comorbidity. <u>Journal of Child Psychology and Psychiatry</u>, <u>34</u>, 1241-1251.

32. Barkley, R.A. (1987). <u>Defiant children: A clinician's manual for parent training</u>. New York: Guilford Press.

33. Boyle, M.H., Offord, D.R., Racine, Y., Fleming, J.E., Szatmari, P., and Sanford, M. (1993). Evaluation of the Revised Ontario Child Health Study scales. <u>Journal of Child Psychology and Psychiatry</u>, <u>34</u>, 189-213.

34. Ullmann, R. K., Sleator, E. K., & Sprague, R. (1984). A new rating scale for diagnosis and monitoring of ADD children. <u>Psychopharmacology Bulletin</u>, <u>20</u>, 160-164.

35. Brandon, K.A., Kehle, T.J., Jeson, W.R., & Clark, E. (1990). Regression, practice, and expectation effects on the Revised Conners Teacher Rating Scale. <u>Journal of Psychoeducational Assessment</u>, <u>8</u>, 456-466.

36. Achenbach, T.M., & Edelbrock, C. (1987). <u>Manual for the Child Behavior Checklist-Youth Self-Report</u>. Burlington: Department of Psychiatry, University of Vermont.

37. Wender, P. H. (1987). <u>s</u>. New York: Oxford University Press.

38. Ward, M. F., Wender, P. H., Reimherr, F. W. (1993). The Wender Utah Rating Scale: An aid in the retrospective diagnosis of childhood attention deficit hyperactivity disorder. <u>American Journal of Psychiatry</u>, <u>150</u>, 885-890.

39. Kovacs, M. (1981). Rating scales to assess depression in school-aged children. <u>Acta Paedopsychiatry</u>, <u>46</u>, 305-315.

40. Reynolds, W.M. (1987). Reynolds Adolescent depression in school-aged children. <u>Acta Paedopsychiatry</u>, <u>46</u>, 305-315.

41. Chiles, J. A., Miller, M. L., & Cox, G. B. (1980). Depression in an adolescent delinquent population. <u>Archives of General Psychiatry</u>, <u>37</u>, 1179-1184.

42. Beck, A.T., Ward, C.H., Mendelson, M., Mack, J., & Erbaugh, J. (1961). An inventory for measuring depression. <u>Archives of General Psychiatry</u>, <u>4</u>, 561-571.

43. Derogatis, L. (1986). <u>Manual for the Symptom Checklist 90 revised (SSCL-90R)</u>. Baltimore: Author.

44. Spitzer, R. L., Williams, J. B. W., Gibbon, M., First, M. B. (1990). <u>Structured clinical interview for DSM-III-R Non-Patient Edition</u> (SCID-NP, Version 1.0). Washington, DC: American Psychiatric Press.

45. Rosvold, H.E., Mirsky, A.F., Sarason, E.D., Bransome, E.D., & Beck, L.H. (1956). A continuous performance test of brain damage. Journal of Consulting Psychology, 20, 343-350.

46. Wechsler, D. (1991). The Wechsler Intelligence Scale for Children Revised (3rd ed.). New York: The Psychological Corporation.

47. Kagan, J. (1966). Reflection-impulsivity: The generality and dynamics of conceptual tempo. Journal of Abnormal Psychology, 71, 17-254.

48. Gordon, M. (1986). How is a computerized attention test used in the diagnosis of attention deficit disorder? Journal of Children in Contemporary Society, 19, 53-64.

49. Corkum, P. V. & Siegel, L. S. (1993). Is the Continuous Performance Task a valuable research tool for use with children with attention-deficit-hyperactivity disorder? Journal of Child Psychology & Psychiatry & Allied Disciplines, 34, 1217-1239.

50. DuPaul, G. J., Anastopoulos, A. D., Shelton, T. L., Guevremont, D. C. Metevia, L. (1992). Multi-method assessment of attention deficit hyperactivity disorder: The diagnostic utility of clinic-based tests. Journal of Clinical Child Psychology, 21, 394-402.

51. Ownby, R.L., & Matthews, C.G. (1985). On the meaning of the WISC-R third factor: Relations to selected neuropsychological measures. Journal of Consulting and Clinical Psychology, 53, 531-534.

52. Grant, D., & Berg, E. (1948). The Wisconsin Card Sort Test: Directions for administrations and scoring. Odessa, FL: Psychological Assessment Resources.

53. Stroop, J.R. (1935). Studies of interference in serial verbal reactions. Journal of Experimental Psychology, 18, 643-662.

54. Kaufman, A.S., & Kaufman, N.L. (1983). Kaufman Assessment Battery for children. Circle Pines, MN: American Guidance Service.

55. Koziol, L.F., & Stout, C.E. (1992). Use of a verbal fluency measure in understanding and evaluating ADHD as an executive function disorder. Perceptual and Motor Skills, 75, 1187-1192.

56. Rich, D., & Taylor, H.G. (1993). Attention deficit hyperactivity disorder. In M.I. Singer, L.T. Singer, & T.M. Anglin (Eds.) Handbook for screening adolescents at psychosocial risk (pp. 333-374). New York: Lexington Books.

57. Silver, L.B. (1992). Attention deficit hyperactivity disorder: A clinical guide to diagnosis and treatment. Washington, DC: American Psychiatric Press, Inc.

58. Moos, R.H., & Moos, B.S. (1986). Family Environment Scale. Palo Alto: Consulting Psychologists.

59. Miller, I.W., Bishop, D.S., Epstein, N.B., & Keitner, G.I. (1985). The McMaster Family Assesment Device: Reliability and validity. Journal of Marital and Family Therapy, 11, 345-356.

60. Moos, R.H., & Moos, B.S. (1988). <u>Life Stressors and Social Resources Inventory: Preliminary manual</u>. Palo Alto: Stanford University and VA Medical Centers.

61. Derogatis, L., & Melilsaratos, N. (1983). The Brief Symptom Inventory: An introductory report. <u>Psychological Medicine, 13</u>, 595-605.

62. Abidin, R.R. (1990). <u>The Parenting Stress Index</u> (3rd ed.) Charlottesville, VA: Pediatric Psychology Press.

63. Lilienfeld, S. O. & Waldman, I. D. (1990). The relation between childhood attention-deficit hyperactivity disorder and adult antisocial behavior reexamined: The problem of heterogeneity. <u>Clinical Psychology Review, 10</u>, 699-725.

64. Pennington, B.F. (1991). <u>Diagnosing learning disorders: A neuropsychological framework</u>. New York: Guilford Press.

65. West, S. A., McElroy, S. L., Strakowski, S. M., Keck, Jr., P. E., McConville, B. J. (1995). Attention deficit hyperactivity disorder in adolescent mania. <u>American Journal of Psychiatry, 152</u>, 271-273.

66. Elia, J., Rapoport, J.L., & Kirby, J. (1993). Pharmacological treatment of attention deficit hyperactivity disorder. In J.L. Matson (Ed.), <u>Handbook of hyperactivity in children</u> (pp. 220-233). Boston: Allyn and Bacon.

67. Sylvester, C. E., & Kruesi, M. J. P. (1994). Child and adolescent psychopharmacotherapy: Progress and pitfalls. <u>Psychiatric Annals, 24</u>, 83-90.

68. Gammon, G.D. & Brown, T.E. (1993). Fluoxetine and methylphenidate in combination for treatment of ADD and comorbid depressive disorder: <u>Journal of Child and Adolescent Psychopharmacology, 3</u>, 1-10.

69. Rapport, M.D., Carlson, G.A., Kelly, K.L., & Pataki, C. (1993). Methylphenidate and desipramine in hospitalized children; Separate and combined effects on cognitive function. <u>Journal of the American Academy of Child and Adolescent Psychiatry, 32</u>, 333-342.

70. Wilens, T.E., Biederman, J., Geist, D.E., Steingard, R., et. al. (1993). Nortriptyline in the treatment of ADHD: A chart review of 58 cases. <u>Journal of the American Academy of Child and Adolescent Psychiatry, 32</u>, 350-353.

71. Wilens, T. E., Biederman, J., Mick, E., Spencer, T. J. (199). A systematic assessment of tricyclic antidepressants in the treatment of adult attention-deficit hyperactivity disorder. <u>Journal of Nervous and Mental Disease, 183</u>, 48-50.

72. Carlson, C. L., & Bunner, M. R. (1993). Effects of methylphenidate on the academic performance of children with attention-deficit hyperactivity disorder and learning disabilities. <u>School Psychology Review, 22</u>, 184-198.

73. Safer, D.J., & Allen, R.P. (1975). Stimulant drug treatment of hyperactive adolescents. <u>Diseases of the Nervous System, 36</u>, 454-457.

74. Wender, P. H., Reimherr, F. W., Wood, D. R., Ward, M. (1985). A controlled study of methylphenidate in the treatment of attention deficit disorder, residual type, in adults. American Journal of Psychiatry, 142, 547-552.

75. Fergusson, D.M., Horwood, L.J., & Lloyd, M. (1993). Early dentine lead levels and subsequent cognitive and behavioral development. Journal of Child Psychology and Psychiatry, 34, 215-227.

76. Feingold, B.F., German, D.F., Brahm, R.M., & Simmers, E. (1973). Adverse reaction to food additives. Paper presented at the Annual meeting of the American Medical Association, New York.

77. Rosén, L.A., Schissel, D., Taylor, & Krein, L. (1993). Nutrition. In J.L. Matson (ed.), Handbook of hyperactivity in children (pp. 282-304). Boston: Allen and Bacon.

78. Boris, M., & Mandel, F.S. (1994). Foods and additives are common causes of attention deficit hyperactivity disorder in children. Annals of Allergy, 72, 462-468.

79. McGee, R., Stanton, W.R., & Sears, M.R. (1993). Allergic disorders and attention dieficit disorders in children. Journal of Abnormal Child Psychology, 21, 79-88.

80. Kagan, J. (1989). Temperamental contributions to social behavior. American Psychologist, 44, 668-674.

81. Fonagy, P., Target, M. (1994). The efficacy of psychoanalysis for children with disruptive disorders. Journal of American Academy of Child and Adolescent Psychiatry, 33, 4555.

82. Cunningham, C.E., & Cappelli, M. (1993). Attention deficit hyperactivity disorder. In A.S. Bellack & M. Hersen (Eds.), Handbook of behavior therapy in the psychiatric setting (pp. 513-540). New York: Plenum Press.

83. Anastopoulos, A.D., Shelton, T.L., DuPaul, G.J., Guevremont, D.C. (1993). Parent training for attention-deficit hyperactivity disorder: Its impact on parent functioning. Journal of Abnormal Child Psychology, 21, 581-596.

84. DuPaul, G.J., & Henningson, P.M. (1993). Peer tutoring effects on the classroom performance of children with attention deficit hyperactivity disorder. School Psychology Review, 22, 132-143.

85. Kolko, D.J., Loar, L.L., Sturnick, D. (1990). Inpatient social cognitive skills training groups with conduct disordered and attention deficit disordered children. Journal of Child Psychology and Psychiatry, 31, 737-748.

86. Pelham, W.E., Carlson, C.L., Sams, S.E., Vallano, G., et.al. (1993). Separate and combined effects of methylphenidate and behavior modification on boys with attention deficit hyperactivity disorder in the classroom. Journal of Consulting and Clinical Psychology, 61, 506-515.

Index

We Want Your Opinion!

Comments about the book: _____
Name of Book

_____

_____

_____

_____

Other titles you want Compact Clinicals to offer:

_____

_____

_____

_____

Please provide your name and address in the space below to be placed on our mailing list.

_____

_____

_____

_____

© Compact Clinicals

Ordering in three easy steps:

Order 24 hours a day: 1(800)408-8830

1   **Please fill out completely:**

Billing/Shipping Information

Individual/Company   Department/Mail Stop
_____

Street Address/P.O. Box
_____

City, State, Zip
_____

Telephone
_____

2   **Here's what I'd like to order:**

Book/Tape Name	Book Qty.	Unit Price	Tape Qty.	Unit Price	Total
Major Depressive Disorder The Latest Assessment and Treatment Strategies		$14.95		$12.95	
Borderline Personality Disorder The Latest Assessment and Treatment Strategies		$14.95		$12.95	
A Condensed Review of the Changes from DSM-III-R to DSM-IV		$16.95	✕		
Conduct Disorders The Latest Assessment and Treatment Strategies		$14.95		$12.95	
Attention Deficit Hyperactivity Disorder The Latest Assessment and Treatment Strategies		$14.95		$12.95	

Subtotal

Tax:Add (6.225% in MO and 6.75% in KS)

Shipping Fee: Add ($3.75 for the first book/tape and $1.00
    for each additional book/tape)

Total Amount

3
    Payment Method:
    ☐ Check enclosed payable to Compact Clinicals
    ☐ Charge: Visa ◯   MasterCard ◯   Name on Card _____
    Signature: _____
    Account #: _____ Exp. Date: _____

Telephone Orders/Toll Free: 1(800)408-8830   Fax Orders to: 1(816)587-7198
Send Postal Orders to: Compact Clinicals, 7205 NW Waukomis Dr., Suite A,
                    Kansas City, MO 64151